POCKET
DICTIONARY *of*
NEW RELIGIOUS
MOVEMENTS

IRVING HEXHAM

InterVarsity Press
Downers Grove, Illinois

InterVarsity Press
P.O. Box 1400, Downers Grove, IL 60515-1426
World Wide Web: www.ivpress.com
E-mail: mail@ivpress.com

InterVarsity Press® is the book-publishing division of InterVarsity Christian Fellowship/
USA®, a student movement active on campus at hundreds of universities, colleges and
schools of nursing in the United States of America, and a member movement of the
International Fellowship of Evangelical Students. For information about local and regional
activities, write Public Relations Dept., InterVarsity Christian Fellowship/USA, 6400
Schroeder Rd., P.O. Box 7895, Madison, WI 53707-7895, or visit the IVCF website at
<www.ivcf.org>.

Cover illustration: Roberta Polfus
ISBN 0-8308-1466-3
Printed in the United States of America ∞

Library of Congress Cataloging-in-Publication Data

Hexham, Irving.
    Pocket dictionary of new religious movements/Irving Hexham.
      p. cm.
    ISBN 0-8308-1466-3 (paper: alk. paper)
    1. Cults—Dictionaries.   2. Sects—Dictionaries.   I. Title.
BP601 .H49 2002
299'.93—dc21
                                                                2001051798

P 19 18 17 16 15 14 13 12 11 10 9 8 7 6 5 4 3 2 1
Y 17 16 15 14 13 12 11 10 09 08 07 06 05 04 03 02

Preface

Finding your way around a new subject can be a daunting task. This dictionary was compiled to help you navigate your religious studies course or identify the various religious groups and ideas you encounter in everyday life. It is based on twenty years of experience in teaching courses on new religions to undergraduates and on extensive archival and field work in Africa, Europe and North America.

My aim throughout has been to produce a book that would be of practical value to the struggling student. So at the outset let me lay out some points you'll want to be aware of.

First, all the terms deal with what sociologists and scholars of religion usually call new religious movements, or NRMs. These are religious groups that the press and members of the public usually call "cults."

Second, information on some items can prove difficult to obtain. Therefore I have addressed each item not according to an evaluation of its overall importance in religious studies but in terms of the difficulty students are likely to encounter in gaining information about it.

Third, I have retained the essentially Christian system of dates—B.C. and A.D.—instead of the increasingly popular B.C.E. ("Before Common Era") and C.E. ("Common Era"). This is because the so-called Common Era is common to Jews and Christians but still excludes Buddhists, Hindus and Muslims. It is therefore a misleading term. For this reason I prefer the traditional Western usage to a modern innovation that does not even have the saving grace that it developed in a homogeneous society.

Fourth, while many of the movements mentioned in this text maintain websites, I have chosen not to include addresses for those sites. As anyone who uses the Internet knows, URLs are constantly changing. So let me just direct you to my own website—"Cults and Religions"

<www.ucalgary.ca/~nurelweb>. There you can find updated links to the websites of groups mentioned in this dictionary as well as additional essays and bibliographical information on the subject of new religious movements.

I wish to acknowledge my debt to my original teacher, Ninian Smart, whose professionalism and enthusiasm for religious studies kindled my own interest. From him I learned the value of empathy and philosophical analysis. Later, from Fred Welbourn, I realized the importance of getting one's hands dirty by studying living religions and not only texts abstracted from their social setting.

I must confess the use of many sources, the most important of which are the following: Geddes MacGregor, *Dictionary of Religion and Philosophy;* Peter A. Angeles, *Dictionary of Philosophy;* S. G. F. Brandon, *A Dictionary of Comparative Religion;* Erwin L. Lueker, *Lutheran Cyclopedia;* J. D. Douglas, *New Bible Dictionary;* Daniel G. Reid, *Dictionary of Christianity in America;* Paul Edward, *The Encyclopedia of Philosophy;* F. L. Cross, *The Oxford Dictionary of the Christian Church;* Lefferts A. Loetscher, *Twentieth-Century Encyclopedia of Religious Knowledge;* Phillip P. Wiener, *Dictionary of the History of Ideas;* Sinclair B. Ferguson and David F. Wright, *New Dictionary of Theology;* Walter A. Elwell, *Evangelical Dictionary of Theology;* Benjamin Walker, *Hindu World;* H. A. R. Gibb and J. H. Kramers, *Shorter Encyclopedia of Islam;* Gordon Melton's various reference works on new religions; Karl Rahner, *Encyclopedia of Theology: The Concise "Sacramentum Mundi";* and handouts provided by my various teachers, especially Colin Lyas, Edward Conze, Bob Morgan, David Catchpole and Jacob Zakkie (James Dickie).

Finally, I hope this text will be judged in terms of its contribution to student needs and its value as a research tool.

A

Aagaard, Johannes (1928-). Professor of religious studies at the University of Aarhus in Denmark who pioneered the study of *new religions in Europe. His work ranges from objective scholarship to writing and editing to *countercult and even *anticult apologetics. He is the coeditor of *Berliner Dialog* and coeditor, with Helle Meldgaard, of *Religious Movements in Europe* (1997).

Abramic religions. Religious traditions that trace their ancestry to the patriarch Abraham. The major religions in this grouping are Christianity, Islam and Judaism. Generally Abramic religions stress (1) the importance of a Creator God who is separate from the world and (2) the duty of humans to obey God.

absolute. A concept popularized by the German philosopher Georg Wilhelm Friedrich Hegel (1770-1831) and used by many philosophers in the nineteenth century to signify self-subsistence, unconditionedness, the ultimate, the first cause or God. It was revived in the twentieth century as a term for deity by various thinkers promoting Eastern, or *yogic, religious ideas. The notion is used in the philosophy of absolute idealism and the philosophical tradition, usually associated with Hegel, that stresses all reality as an idea of God or the Absolute.

absurd. A term used in the philosophy known as *existentialism to speak of the human condition. Many *new religions are based on existential ideas.

active imagination. A Jungian psychotherapeutic technique of introversion that is said to allow individuals direct access to the *unconscious world of memories and dreams. Using an analogy with archaeology, Carl *Jung argued that the imagination may be used "to make excavations into the phylogeny of the soul." The idea comes from *theosophists, who believed that the ancestral past could be contacted directly through the imagination.

acupuncture. An ancient Chinese medical technique that involves placing needles into specific areas of the body. Some doctors believe that the procedure stimulates natural processes and releases body chemicals that speed recovery. In Eastern religions and in holistic medicine, however, its effects are often given an *occult explanation. *See also* alternative medicine.

Adamski, George (1891-1965). American *occultist and promoter of *pseudoscience who popularized the idea of UFOs, or flying saucers, through his claim to have been contacted by "space brothers." The author of one science fiction novel, *Pioneers in Space,* he became famous through his book *Flying Saucers Have Landed* (1953), which he wrote with Desmond Leslie. This book draws on *theosophical sources and propagates the basic ancient astronautics theory found in later writers such as Erich von *Däniken and Shirley *Maclaine. Adamski's work is important in understanding the *New Age movement.

adventism. The belief that Christ's return is imminent and will inaugurate a millennial kingdom. (*See* chiliasm; millenarian movement; millennialism.) Throughout Christian history various adventist groups have arisen. In the nineteenth century, however, they flourished in America as the result of the teachings of a Baptist minister, William *Miller. Out of his prophetic conferences various adventist movements developed, the most famous being the *Seventh-day Adventists. The ideas generated by this dynamic movement influenced many orthodox Christian groups as well as gave birth to a large number of unorthodox groups, such as the *Jehovah's Witnesses and *Christadelphians.

Aetherius Society. One of the earliest *new religions involving the claim that its founder—in this case, George *King—was in communication with the inhabitants of a UFO. In 1954 King began talking about his communications with the *ascended master Aetherius, whom he claimed represented an interplanetary parliament. A small group of devotees quickly gathered around King in London, England, and in 1956 he founded the Aetherius Society. Three years later he moved to Los Angeles, where the society flourished. King's books sold well and his message seems to have inspired numerous other "contactees," all with slightly different versions of the extraterrestrials' teachings. Among the many groups to be indirectly inspired by King's message was the *Heaven's Gate community.

African independent churches. Since the late nineteenth century, thousands of *new religious movements have developed in Africa. Almost all of these claim to be Christian, and yet they reject traditional missionary churches and attempt to incorporate many traditional African beliefs and practices into their worship and theology. Most of these churches are thoroughly Christian, although some are clearly closer to *African traditional religions than to Christianity. Various scholars—including Lutheran bishop Bengt Sundkler in *Bantu Prophets in South Africa* (1948) and Anglican theologian Fred Welbourn in *East African Rebels* (1961)—have convincingly argued that many African independent churches originated as a result of paternalism and sometimes outright racism on the part of white missionaries and colonial church leaders. Therefore, in assessing the *orthodoxy of such groups, the educational level and social experience and intent of the leaders and followers are important (if neglected) factors. The necessity of this consideration is pointed out in a story told by Bishop Sundkler of the time he challenged an African *prophet and church leader about the man's understanding of the Trinity as expressed in his church's hymns. To his great surprise, the prophet admitted that the theology expressed in some of the hymns was clearly unorthodox. But he went on to say, "I didn't realize the problem until you just pointed it out to me a few moments ago. We are simple people, bishop, who love Jesus. But we lack education and value friends like yourself."

African Israel Church Nineveh. An East African independent church that grew out of a revival movement inspired by Canadian Pentecostal missionaries in Tanzania in 1927. The church itself was founded by Paul David Zakayo Kivuli (1896-1974) in Kenya in 1940 after a dispute over the paternalistic attitude of a white missionary. It obtained its present name in 1956. In their classic study *A Place to Feel at Home* (1966), F. B. Welbourn and B. A. Ogot argue that in intent and in the aims of its leaders, the church is an essentially orthodox Christian church adapted to African society through an emphasis on healing, dreams and use of the Hebrew Bible. *See also* African independent churches.

African traditional religions. A diverse body of traditions located on the African continent. Some African traditional religions involve a High God, some many gods; some seem almost atheistic, placing all their emphasis on placating ancestors. The quest for healing, both physical and spiritual, is a major factor in most African traditional religions, as is release from and protection against witchcraft. African religions are frequently treated as "the same," perhaps because of a subconscious belief that they are essentially "primitive," while other geographically clustered traditions, such as the religions of India, represent profound philosophical traditions. But even as no serious scholar suggests that the religions of India (Buddhism, the Hindu tradition, Jainism, etc.) can be treated as essentially one religion, even though they share many similar concepts (e.g., karma, meditation, yoga), African traditions are actually highly complex and deserve much better treatment than they have received from Western scholars in the past. Works like Edward E. Evans-Pritchard's *Nuer Religion* (1956), Paul Parin, Fritz Morgenthaler and Goldy Parn-Matthey's *Fear Thy Neighbor*

As Thyself (1980) and Wyatt MacGaffey's *Religion and Society in Central Africa* (1986) bring out the richness of African traditions, while F. B. Welbourn's concise *Atoms and Ancestors* (1968) remains the best general introduction.

Age of Aquarius. Astrological theory of "star ages" during which the earth and its inhabitants are subject to astral influences. Each star age is said to last approximately twenty-two hundred years. The last star age began shortly before the birth of Christ and is now believed to be coming to an end as the new *occult Age of Aquarius dawns. The term became popular in the 1960s through the musical stage play *Hair*. *See also* astrology.

agnosticism. The position that all knowledge of such entities as a divine being, immortality and a supernatural world is impossible. The word is attributed to the nineteenth-century skeptic T. H. *Huxley and is used by people who wish to avoid professing dogmatic *atheism.

Ahmad, Hadhrat Mirza Ghulam (1835-1908). Born in the Punjab, he claimed the dignity of a *Mahdi and founded the *Ahmadiyya *sect of Islam. His teachings are set out in *The Arguments of the Ahmadiyya*, the first volume of which appeared in 1880. Orthodox Muslims regard him and his writings as heretical.

Ahmadiyya. An Islamic *sect found among non-Arab Muslims and considered heretical by the orthodox. Established in nineteenth-century India by Hadhrat Mirza Ghulam *Ahmad, Ahmadiyya began as a *revitalization movement within *Islam. But in 1889 Ahmad claimed to have received a *revelation giving him the right to receive homage. He claimed to be the *Mahdi, or world teacher, expected by Zoroastrians, Hindus and Buddhists. He said he was an *avatar of *Krishna, who had come in the spirit of Muhammad. Defending his beliefs against the orthodox, he held that Sura 61 in the Qur'an speaks of him. He claimed his personality had been merged with that of Muhammad, so to call him a *prophet did not contradict Islamic belief. He is believed to have performed signs and miracles as proof of his authority. After his death, his son Bashir al-din Mahmud Ahmad was appointed his successor. The movement's missions have spread to many parts of the world and its teachings can be found in the *Teachings of Islam* (Ahmad, 1963). Regarding Christianity, Ghulam Ahmad taught that Jesus was crucified but taken from the cross alive and resuscitated. Jesus then went to Kashmir, where he preached, married and died at the age of 120.

Aladura. A movement of *African independent churches that includes the Church of the Lord Aladura and the Cherubim and Seraphim churches. This movement grew out of several prophetic movements in the Niger delta during the 1890s and was strongly affected by the 1918 influenza epidemic, from which a number of African independent churches came into existence. Aladura has since spread throughout West Africa, with branches in Europe and North America. These churches combine an emphasis on prayer and healing with African custom and the acceptance of what is at times a somewhat confused and yet, in its intent, essentially orthodox Christian theology.

Albigenses. A Christian heretical *sect named after the city of Albi in the south of France that is often identified by modern *occult groups as a forerunner to their own beliefs. It arose in the eleventh century and flourished in the twelfth and thirteenth centuries before being brutally suppressed by the Inquisition. It professed a form of Manichaean dualism that regarded Christ as an *angel with a phantom body, proclaimed that the Roman Catholic Church was corrupt and taught a form of *esoteric and *occult knowledge as the means of salvation.

alchemy. Originally a form of early chemistry developed in ancient Egypt. It led to attempts to transmute metals, such as turning lead into gold, and by the Greco-Roman period had acquired a mystical dimension. Alchemy flourished as a bogus science in medieval Christian and Islamic cultures. It fell out of favor with the Reformation and the rise of modern science but has seen a revival as a form of New Age knowledge linked to holistic health and alien intelligence.

Alexander technique. A method of developing good body posture and correct breathing that has had spectacular results with certain forms of illness and among the physically disabled. Although essentially a secular therapy, it has sometimes been incorporated into some forms of *alternative medicine and been given *occult significance.

alien abduction. The claim by numerous individuals that they were abducted by aliens in spacecraft. This claim often leads to the founding of a new *UFO religion. After extensive research, psychologists now believe that these experiences are the result of what they call "sleep paralysis" (see *The Skeptical Inquirer*, May 1998).

alienation. An English word originating in the fourteenth century and used to describe an action of estranging or a state of estrangement. In modern usage its meanings include (1) a cutting off from another, such as God; (2) a breakdown of relations between persons or groups; (3) the action of transferring the ownership of anything to another; and (4) loss of connection with one's own deepest feelings and needs. G. W. F. Hegel and Karl Marx argued that what is alienated is an essential part of human nature and that the process of alienation must be seen historically. Ludwig *Feuerbach described God as the product of human alienation in the sense of God's being a projection of the highest human attributes from people to a divine being. Karl Marx said people create themselves by creating their world but that in class-based society they are alienated from their essential nature. The term has been adopted by many *new religions to express the essence of the human condition.

allegorical interpretation. Interpreting Scripture by detecting spiritual meanings beneath the surface meaning of a text. This form of interpretation was popular in the early Christian church and survives today in some evangelical and fundamentalist circles. The method reads a text, presupposing that its apparent or literal meaning conceals another "deeper" or "true" meaning. For instance, instead of treating the story of David in historical terms, allegorical interpretation sees his life story in terms of the pilgrimage of the soul toward final salvation.

allegory. A sustained or prolonged metaphor. The use of language to convey a deeper and different meaning from that which appears on the surface.

alternative medicine. Traditional medicines and modern therapies existing outside the modern medical establishment. The term includes such things as herbalism, *homeopathy and various techniques of *spiritual healing.

Ama-Nazaretha. Known as Nazarites, the largest Zulu *African independent church movement. The theology of the Nazarites is a blend of Christian and Zulu beliefs. Their founder, Isaia *Shembe, was a Baptist, but his followers have tended to deify him and to see him as a black Messiah. The group was founded in 1911 and split into two rival camps following the death of Isaia Shembe's son, Johannes Galilee *Shembe, in 1976. At least one branch of the movement exists in Los Angeles and another in New York, while several branches are to be found in Europe.

American Family Foundation (AFF). The leading *anticult organization in America. It was founded in 1979 by a group of parents concerned about the conversion of their children to *new religions. It is supported by psychologists, anticult activists and ex-cult members, many of whom renounced their membership in new religions during deprogramming sessions. The AFF publishes various informational booklets, a regular newsletter called *The Cult Observer* and an academic journal called *Cultic Studies Journal*. *See also* cult; new religious movements.

AMORC. The Ancient and Mystical Order of the Rosae Crucis. It was founded in 1915 by the folklore specialist and occult writer H. Spencer Lewis. It is now based in California and has groups scattered throughout the world. It has tremendous influence in promoting *New Age-type ideas in places like Africa through its correspondence courses and other propaganda. Essentially the movement is a soft *occultism that emphasizes spiritual *evolution, *reincarnation, health, wealth and happiness.

amulet. Magical object used to give protection against evil forces. Amulets are often worn on clothing or as jewelry. Larger amulets may be used to protect buildings or special places. *See also* magic.

Ananda Community. Founded in 1968 by an American, J. Donald Walters, who called himself Swami Kriyananda. This is one of the more successful *New Age-type communities to have developed out of the 1960s *counterculture. The community has around three hundred members and finds its inspiration in the work of Swami Paramhansa *Yogananda.

Ananda Marga. A controversial Hindu *revitalization movement. Founded in 1955 by Ananda *Murti (or Anandamurti), it has over five million members. It is based on the practice of *tantric *yoga and teaches that violence is a legitimate means of establishing a Hindu society. The movement is highly critical of Indian democracy, which it claims is a sham due to widespread illiteracy and poverty. Critics accuse the movement of murdering its enemies and having unacceptable political ambitions.

anarchism. A political doctrine propounded by Pierre Joseph Proudhon (1809-1865) and Mikhail Bakunin (1814-1876) holding that all forms of authority and civil government are bad. In its extreme form it supports violent revolution and terrorism to destroy all structures of authority. Numerous *new religions—particularly those of Russian origin, such as the *Dukhobors—have anarchist tendencies.

androgyny. A state in which male and female characteristics exist in one person and sexual differentiation has not arisen. This was highly prized in some *Gnostic religious systems as more perfect than either male or female. Such systems disparage human sexuality by emphasizing an unworldly spirituality.

angels. Originally, messengers of God in Christianity, Judaism and Islam. Angels are believed to be divided between good angels who continue to serve God and evil angels who have rebelled against God. Muslims believe that God dictated the Qur'an to Muhammad through the agency of an angel. Ama-Nazarites believe that their hymns were first sung by the angels and then recited by Isaia *Shembe. (*See* Ama-Nazaretha.) Angels are also found in Zoroastrianism, Manichaeism and some forms of Chinese religion.

animism. A term often used (misleadingly) to characterize African and other nonliterate religious systems and the belief in *nature spirits. The term was first introduced by Sir Edward B. Tylor (1832-1917) as a "minimum definition" of religion. He argued that from sleep experiences, such as dreams, "primitive man" developed the idea of *anima*, or the spiritual principle that animates material objects. Thus rivers, trees, stones, the sun, moon and sacred objects such as masks were said to possess spiritual power caused by the indwelling of spirit beings. These ideas, Tylor argued, produced fear that led to worship and the development of religion. Today the term *animism* has fallen into disuse among serious scholars of religion, although it is still retained by some missiologists. The reason most academics have rejected this term is because it fails to recognize the highly complex nature of many nonliterate religions that do not rely on simplistic notions of the spiritual world. The idea behind animism is in fact historically a racist one, which assumes that nonliterate peoples lack the intellectual ability to develop complex religions and philosophies. It also imposes one system of beliefs on what are usually far more diverse systems, thus distorting what people actually believe. Abandoning the term to allow for the recognition of the complexity of religious systems is advisable. The British anthropologist Edward E. Evans-Pritchard (1902-1973) did more than anyone else to dispel simplistic notions about "primitive religion" in books such as *Witchcraft, Oracles and Magic Among the Azande* (1936) and *Nuer Religion* (1956).

ankh. The ancient Egyptian religious symbol of life formed by a cross with a loop at the top. (*See* Egyptian religions.) Today it is often used by so-called *New Age religious groups and is a popular design in jewelry.

anthropocentrism. The viewpoint expressed in Protagoras's saying that "man is the measure of all things." It is today associated with humanism. Recently it has been used by people in the environmental movement as a critique of views that give greater value to humankind over the rest of nature.

anthroposophy. Although little known in North America, this is a major *new religion in Europe, particularly Germany, that promotes a Christianized form of *theosophy. It was founded by Rudolf *Steiner in 1912. The group is best known through its Waldorf schools, which incorporate Steiner's ideas into their educational philosophy. They also manufacture holistic cosmetics and various other items of a similar nature that are used to promote the group's views. Although more sympathetic to Christian teachings than theosophy, Steiner's views are essentially a form of *neopaganism, with *occult and Eastern influences incorporated into an intellectual system that strongly emphasizes aesthetics and cultural creativity. Although not well known in the English-speaking world, anthroposophy has considerable influence through theosophical groups where Steiner's ideas circulate.

antichrist. The word used by the author of the Johannine epistles for those who deny Christ (1 Jn 2:18-22; 2 Jn 7). The New Testament elsewhere implies that at the end of human history an antichrist figure will appear to wage war on the church (compare the man of lawlessness, 2 Thess 2:1-12; the beast that arises from the sea, Rev 11:7; 13:1-10; 16:12-16; 17; 19:19-21). This belief has fueled many *millenarian movements.

anticult movement. A grassroots movement that invokes the notion of *brainwashing to explain conversion to new religions. The movement originated in North America in the 1970s, involving parents, friends and ex-members of *new religious movements. Through the skillful use of media, especially television, it has become a powerful social force and is seen by most sociologists of religions and religious studies scholars as an essentially antireligious movement that is a threat to religious freedom. The anticult movement bases its theories about brainwashing ultimately on the work of British psychiatrist William *Sargent, as popularized by Flo Conway and Jim Siegelman in their book *Snapping* (1978). The major objection to the methods used by the anticult movement is that its criteria for defining a "cult" are based on correlates (that is, incidental attributes) and not real definitions. Consequently these criteria usually apply with equal force to the activities of evangelical Christians, Roman Catholics and so on. (*See* Tnevnoc cult.) The problem can also be seen if one applies notions like "isolation from family" and "restrictions on sexual behavior" to such things as Christian summer camps or short-term mission activities. *See also* cult.

anti-Semitism. An attitude of hostility toward Jewish people and Judaism. Religiously, it has been linked to the belief that the Jews as a race were responsible for the death of Jesus. This belief has been repudiated by most Christian theologians and was rejected by the Second Vatican Council (1965-1966). In the nineteenth century various anti-Semitic groups formed Nordic religions or sought to free people from the "imperialistic hold" of "Jewish-Christianity." Later, German new religions such as the *Ludendorff Bewegung made anti-Semitism a key element in their teachings, while some mainline theologians, like Rudolf Kittel, sought to prove that Jesus wasn't really Jewish at all. There are various kinds of anti-Semitism, ranging from a mild dislike of Jews or Judaism to the virulent exterministic type embraced by some *Nazis. Religious anti-Semitism seeks to free Christianity from its Jewish roots; it took on its modern form with deists like Thomas *Paine, who judged the Bible an immoral book. These attitudes were involved in the early development of *biblical criticism and many *new religious movements.

apocalypse. This term can refer to (1) the last book of the New Testament, the book of Revelation, which is attributed to the apostle John; (2) the ancient Hebrew and Christian visionary literature generally; or (3) the events surrounding the end of the world. Many writers try to produce a philosophy of history from the Bible, foretelling the end of the world, in works that often inspire new religious groups, such as the *Jehovah's Witnesses.

apocalyptic fiction. A form of writing that promotes ideas about biblical *prophecy through fiction. It first became popular in German Pietist circles in the late eighteenth century. Today this genre is enjoying a resurgence among *Mormons and evangelical Christians. The advantage of this type of writing is that, unlike more theological books, it cannot be refuted when the predictions of the author fail to materialize. After all, it is only fiction. Nevertheless, many people take it to be teaching the truth. *See also* apocalypse.

apocalyptic literature. A genre of literature distinguished principally by its mysterious allusions to the signs preceding the events to occur in the last days of world history. The Society for Biblical Literature has defined apocalyptic literature as a genre of revelatory literature with a narrative framework where *revelation is mediated by otherwordly beings to human recipients disclosing a transcendental reality that is temporal (eschatological salvation) and spatial (involving another supernatural world). These are religious works written in figurative language and are often difficult to interpret. *See also* apocalypse.

apocalypticism. Belief in the imminent end of the world or other impending disasters as a result of divine judgment. *See also* apocalypse.

apocrypha. In Greek this word means "hidden things." It has been applied to both Jewish and Christian writings that were excluded from the official canon of Scripture.

Apocryphal New Testament. A collection of writings that the early church deemed as either nonauthoritative for Christian teaching or as teaching error and thus did not adopt as part of the Christian canon of Scripture. In recent years apocryphal literature, such as the Gospel of Thomas, has become popular among alternate religious groups and has formed a basis for many *New Age beliefs. Many extravagant claims have been made about apocryphal writings, but the truth is that most were written well into the second century A.D. and lack all historical connection to the historical Jesus and the apostolic faith.

apollonian. The rational, harmonious and orderly. A term used by Friedrich *Nietzsche to describe one tradition of Greek art. The other tradition he described as dionysian. These terms are often used to describe different aspects of new religions, particularly the contrast between highly controlled groups and free-flowing, spontaneous religious movements.

Applewhite, Marshall Herff (1927-1997). Known to his followers as "Do" or "Bo," he was the cofounder, with Bonnie *Nettles, of the *Heaven's Gate movement that committed mass suicide in 1997. He was a music teacher and college professor who became involved with *theosophical teachings and various *occult influences before abandoning his work to become an itinerant preacher of *UFO beliefs.

Arcane School. The organization established in 1923 by Alice A. *Bailey to propagate a form of *theosophy and the teachings of the *Great White Brotherhood. Originally part of the *Theosophical Society proper, Bailey clashed with Annie *Besant over Besant's belief that Jiddu *Krishnamurti was the expected world savior. Instead she received spiritualist communications promising the return of Christ in the form of the Buddhist *bodhisattva Maitreya. In recent years Benjamine Creme has claimed that he is the fulfillment of this *prophecy, but despite short-term publicity in the early 1970s and again in the 1980s, few people have taken him seriously. Through its many books and writings, the Arcane School has been a major influence on the *New Age movement.

archetype. A notion used by *Plato to signify the original form of things as contrasted with their appearance in the world. It was adopted by Carl G. *Jung and Ludwig *Klages as a term for the collective representation of symbols found in art and dreams and has been popular in many psychologically based new religions.

Arianism. A Christian *heresy named after its proponent *Arius, who maintained that Christ, the Son of God, was created and not fully God, eternal with the Father. Arius was a thoroughgoing Greek rationalist who inherited the almost universally held Logos Christology of the eastern Roman Empire. He contended that God was immutable and unknowable; therefore, Christ had to be a being made by God as the first in the created order. The orthodox counterattack on Arianism pointed out that Arian theology reduced Christ to a demigod and in effect introduced *polytheism into Christianity. In February 325 Arius was condemned as a heretic at a synod in Antioch. The Council of Nicaea, which met in May 325, condemned Arius and his teachings. But instead of resolving the issues, the council launched an empire-wide christological debate during which it often seemed that Arianism would triumph as the dominant form of Christianity. Only after a hundred years of heated debate did *orthodoxy emerge triumphant. Today a form of Arianism has been revived among *Unitarians and the *Jehovah's Witnesses. Historically baseless claims are also made by various *occult groups about Arianism as a persecuted source of occult knowledge.

Arius (c. 256-336). An archheretic of the early church. Arius seems to have been a highly successful preacher and was revered for his asceticism. Arius appears to have written little, preferring instead to embody his teachings in popular songs. He rejected the orthodox definition of the deity of Christ, the Trinity and related doctrines, replacing them with a form of subordination that made Christ the first created being but not God. *See* Arianism.

Armageddon. The name used in Revelation 16:16 for the site of the final battle between the forces of good and evil. Although the Bible says little about Armageddon, it has become the subject of intense speculation among *heretical groups and other groups on the fringe of *orthodoxy. *See also* apocalypticism.

Armstrong, Garner Ted (1930-). The son of Herbert W. *Armstrong and for many years his apparent successor as leader of the *Worldwide Church of God. In the early 1970s a series of allegations about his sexual infidelities forced him to leave the church to establish his own rival organization, which has remained essentially Arian in its doctrine.

Armstrong, Herbert W. (1909-1986). A popular radio and television preacher who founded the *Worldwide Church of God, Ambassador College and the well-known magazine *The Plain Truth.* He promoted a form of Arian theology laced with an Americanized version of *British

Israelism and fortified with a strong premillennial *eschatology. Following the expulsion of his son Garner Ted Armstrong and Herbert's own death, the group became increasingly orthodox in its theology and accepted an evangelical statement of faith in 1997.

Arya Samaj. Hindu reform movement founded by *Swami Dayananda Saraswati in 1870. The movement embraces *monotheism and rejects the worship of images. It claims that the four main *Vedas are the eternal Word of God, embracing all true knowledge either of science or religion. Members of Arya Samaj reject many ancient Hindu social practices, such as the suicide of widows, and give women a greater role than they enjoy in most other Hindu movements.

Aryans. A *Sanskrit term meaning "the Noble Ones" and used to refer to an Indo-European-speaking people who settled in northern India and Iran in the second millennium B.C. In the nineteenth century there was great interest in and debate about Aryan religion and languages. This term was picked up by Madame *Blavatsky and various members of the *Theosophical Society as a key term in their understanding of human history. In the twentieth century *Nazi propagandists used the term to promote their own views about racial purity and to distinguish themselves from Jews.

ascended masters. A term popularized by *theosophy that refers to supposed superhuman beings who are said to guide human destiny. They are often depicted as living in remote places like Tibet or, more recently, on other planets or in UFOs, from which they telepathically communicate with selected human beings. *See also* trance channeling.

astrology. The ancient belief that individual and national destinies are influenced by the stars. The role of the stars in the life of individuals is known as "natal astrology," while "mundane astrology" deals with the fate of nations and concepts like the *Age of Aquarius. Although popular in many cultures in the past and influential even today, astrology was discredited in the seventeenth century by the rise of modern science and the complete failure of a series of well-publicized predictions by prominent astrologers.

atheism. A system of belief that denies there is a God. The term originally was used in Greece of all those who, whether they believed in a god or not, disbelieved in the official gods of the state. The philosopher Socrates was the classic exponent of such unbelief. In the Roman Empire the term was applied to Christians, but sometimes Christians (like the church father Polycarp) would turn the term against their persecutors. Until the term *agnosticism* came into general use in the nineteenth century, atheism was popularly used to describe those who thought the existence of God an unprovable thesis. A remarkable number of advocates of *new religions, such as Annie *Besant, moved from atheism or *agnosticism to become advocates of some form of Eastern spirituality or *neopaganism.

Atlantis. In his dialogue *Timaeus* *Plato mentions an evil people whose city was destroyed by an earthquake that submerged it under the sea. For at least four hundred years after he wrote *Timaeus*, Plato's story was recognized as a parable. Later, some Roman writers began to take it literally. But it was not until the nineteenth century, with the work of Ignatius T. T. *Donnelly, that the idea of such a lost civilization became widespread. From Donnelly it was adapted and given *occult significance by Helena *Blavatsky and has since become a part of the stock-in-trade of occult and *New Age writers such as Shirley *Maclaine, who use it as an apologetic device to promote their claims. In fact, the uncritical acceptance of these claims is one of the weaknesses of New Age writings.

Atman. A key concept in the Hindu tradition for the individualization of reality. It is often translated as "soul" but actually means something rather different and is more akin to the essence of life or fundamental self. In some *Upanishads and *Vedanta, Atman is identified with *Brahman.

audience cults. A term coined by sociologist Rodney *Stark to refer to religious movements that exist as seminars, lecture series or similar events where a speaker, *trance channeler or guru addresses an audience, who often pay for the privilege of hearing the master. After the event, the attendees return home without joining a movement. *See also* cult.

Aum Shinri Kyo. A fanatical Japanese *new religion blending *shamanistic practices, *New Age-type beliefs and *meditation. The leader of the group, Shoko Asahara, is regarded as a messianic figure by his adherents. The group is accused of carrying out a Sarin gas attack on the Tokyo subway on March 22, 1995.

Aurobindo, Sri (1872-1950). Founder of a vigorous Hindu reform and missionary movement. He was educated in England and served the British in India until he was arrested for alleged support of rebels. In jail he had a mystical experience, which resulted in his devoting the rest of his life to religion. In his book *The Life Divine* he seeks to interpret the Hindu tradition in terms of *evolutionary theory in a manner similar to that of the Jesuit Teilhard de Chardin. He taught what he called "integral yoga," which integrated spiritual and practical disciplines. (*See* yoga.) In the 1920s he was joined by a French female convert, Mira Richards (1878-1973), whom he eventually called "the Mother" and with whom he is said to have practiced various forms of *tantra, or spiritual exercises of a sexual nature. After his death, "the Mother" took over and ran his ashram in Pondicherry, which, unlike most ashrams, accommodated married as well as single people and made many concessions to modern technology. *See also* Auroville.

Auroville. A model community that has influenced *New Age thinkers. Founded in India as an international village based on the teachings of Sri *Aurobindo, it was designed and run by Mira Richards (1878-1973), who was known as "the Mother."

avatar. A Hindu term meaning "descent," signifying the manifestation of a god on earth in human or animal form.

avidya. A Hindu term meaning "ignorance," which explains the endless cycle of birth and rebirth that binds humans to the wheel of existence.

Ayur-veda. A collection of medieval Hindu manuscripts containing medical knowledge and magical ideas. They have greatly influenced Eastern medical practices and are now popularized by some advocates of holistic medicine. *See also* alternative medicine.

B

Baha'i Faith. A *new religious movement originating from Islam and considered heretical by orthodox Muslims. It was founded in Persia by Baha' Ullah (1817-1892), who suffered imprisonment and exile for his beliefs. Toward the end of his life Baha' Ullah lived at Bahji (near Acre), where he wrote *Kitab-i-ikan* (Book of Certitude). This is the basic book of laws and teachings that in many ways provides the doctrinal basis of the religion. In addition to this major work, Baha' Ullah wrote numerous other books. In his religion God is held to be transcendent and unknowable but to make himself manifest by his creation and especially by *prophets, who are a mirror in which God, his will and attributes are reflected. The movement seeks universal peace, holds to the unity of the human race, advocates removal of prejudice, teaches that all religions have an essential unity and prays for the dead. After Baha' Ullah's death, his son, 'Abbas Effendi (Abdu'l-Baha), was recognized as the interpreter of his father's writings and undertook missionary work in Europe and America. The movement has spread widely in Europe, America and Africa and in Eastern countries. The administrative center is at Haifa, Israel.

Bailey, Alice (1880-1949). English *occultist. At the age of fifteen Bailey had a vision of an entity who she said was Christ but who she later, under *theosophical influence, decided was a *mystic teacher, Koot Hoomi. In later life she claimed to have contact with another "master"—Djwhal Khul, a Tibetan, who dictated books through her by automatic writing. After a dispute with the *Theosophical Society in 1920, she founded the *Arcane School. Her most important idea was the coming of a new world master who would unite East and West. Her books include *The Unfinished Autobiography* (1951), *Initiation: Human and Solar* (1922) and *A Treatise on White Magic* (1934).

Ballard, Edna Anne Wheeler (1886-1971). American *occultist. Ballard was cofounder with her husband, Guy *Ballard, of the Saint Germain Foundation and leader of the I-Am movement.

Ballard, Guy (1878-1939). American *occultist. In 1930, while hiking on Mount Shasta in California, Ballard had an encounter with an entity he called Saint Germain. During the remaining years of his life, he and his wife, Edna *Ballard, promoted the teachings of Saint Germain and other spirit beings identified as *ascended masters.

Barker, Eileen (1938-). Leading British sociologist of religion and wife of a well-loved BBC classical music radio host. She is the founder of *INFORM and former dean of social science at the prestigious London School of Economics and Political Science. Professor Barker's study of the *Unification Church, *The Making of a Moonie* (1984), led to her vilification by members of the *anticult movement. Her other works include *New Religious Movements: A Practical Introduction* (1989), which was published by Her Majesty's Stationery Office, the official publisher of the British government. She received further recognition from the British government in February 2000 when she was inducted into the Order of the British Empire by the queen.

Batson, Gregory (1904-1980). British anthropologist. His work *Steps to an Ecology of Mind* (1972), in which he speculated about spiritual reality, played an important role in the development of many *new religions in the 1970s as well as the *New Age movement of the 1980s.

Benda, Julien (1867-1956). French rationalist philosopher and novelist. Benda strongly opposed the philosophical system of Henri *Bergson, which sought to spiritualize *evolution. Benda's work *The Treason of the Intellectuals* (1928) was a prophetic analysis of *fascism and the dangers implicit in certain types of idealist philosophy that often provide a basis for *New Age religions.

Bennett, John G. (1897-1974). Popularizer of the Javanese religious movement *Subud in the West. He was a former disciple of George *Gurdjieff and the author of *Concerning Subud* (1958) and other books.

Berg, Moses David (1919-1994). Founder of the *Children of God movement. Berg began his career as a Pentecostal preacher whose spiritual revelations and prophecies led him further and further from *orthodoxy. In his writings he claimed to have received revelations from a host of spiritual beings, including creatures he called "the Abominable Snowman" and "the Pied Piper." These revelations led him to advocate polygamy, a sexual recruitment of new members known as "flirty fishing" and various other questionable sexual practices. He was known as "Mo" to his followers.

Berger, Peter L. (1934-). Austrian-American sociologist best known for his work on the social construction of reality. Many of Berger's ideas have been interpreted to imply relativism—an interpretation that Berger strongly repudiates. His best-known works are *Invitation to Sociology* (1963), *The Social Construction of Reality* (1966, with Thomas Luckmann) and *The Social Reality of Religion* (1967). More recently he has written *The War Against the Family* (1984), in collaboration with his wife, Brigitte Berger, and various books on religion, economics and social theory, such as *Pyramids of Sacrifice* (1974).

Bergson, Henri Louis (1859-1941). French philosopher. Bergson's theories of cosmic evolution have inspired various religious thinkers who have contributed to the growth of process theology and various *new religions that spiritualize the theory of *evolution. His best-known philosophical work is *Creative Evolution* (1907). *See* emergent evolution.

Besant, Annie Wood (1847-1933). English Theosophist. Born of evangelical parents, she married a pious but dull clergyman whom she eventually divorced. Her subsequent religious pilgrimage led from Anglicanism to *atheism to *spiritualism and eventually to *Theosophy. In England she was notorious for her affair with Charles Bradlaugh, a non-Christian member of Parliament, and their promotion of radical causes, including birth control. After her conversion to Theosophy (as taught by Helena *Blavatsky), Besant in 1889 moved to India, where she established a number of educational institutions, including the Central Hindu College (1898) and the University of India (1907). She played an important role in agitating for Indian independence from British rule and was active in the Indian National Congress and was even elected its president. She proclaimed her adopted son, Jiddu *Krishnamurti, a new messiah, but he later repudiated this view. After the death of Helena Blavatsky, Besant became the president of the *Theosophical Society. Her works include *The Ancient Wisdom* (1897) and *The Religious Problems of India* (1902).

Bhagavad-Gita. Hindu scripture. Literally translated "The Song of the Lord," the Bhagavad-Gita is probably the most popular book of *Hindu scripture in the West. It forms part of the great Indian epic, the Mahabharata, which can be dated to somewhere between 200 B.C. and A.D. 200. For many modern Hindus it represents the essence of their religion, with its message that there are many ways to salvation. It consists of a long dialogue between the hero Arjuna and his chariot driver, who (unknown to Arjuna) is really the Lord *Krishna in human form. On the eve of the battle of Kuruksetra, Arjuna has scruples about the prospect of killing his fellow men, some of whom are his kinsmen, but he is told by Krishna that he must perform his duty in a disinterested way appropriate to his caste as a warrior. The Buddhist scholar Edward *Conze and others have argued that the devotional tone of the Gita reflects the influence of Christianity and that it was probably written to counter Christian teachings.

Bhagwan Sri Rajneesh, Chandra Mohan (1931-1991). Founder of the *new religion called *Osho. Bhagwhan Sri Rajneesh was an Indian university teacher with a *Jain background and an M.A. in philosophy. He studied various religions and Western teachers, including George *Gurdjieff and humanistic psychology, and in 1953 founded his own new religion, Osho. He resigned from teaching in 1966 to devote himself to developing his religion based on a technique he called "dynamic meditation." His beliefs incorporated elements from everything he read but endorsed no existing tradition. Deliberately appealing to the rich, he attracted a huge following and in 1981 moved to America, where he founded a large commune, Rajneeshpuram, in eastern Oregon. In a dramatic flight he left America in 1983 after one of his followers tried to assassinate a local district attorney.

bhakti. A term meaning "devotion" and denoting movements within Indian religions, especially Hinduism, that emphasize the love of God or the gods. Bhakti is the loving submission of the believer to the deity as a means of grace and salvation. The *Hare Krishna movement is probably the best-known bhakti movement in the West.

biblical criticism. A type of academic inquiry that arose in the eighteenth century among *deists and gained academic respectability through German universities in the nineteenth century. In its origins

biblical criticism was closely linked to the *anti-Semitism of Thomas
*Paine and other deists who judged biblical stories by their own mo-
rality, leading them to pronounce the Bible an "immoral" book and the
Jews a "wicked people." Later scholars developed biblical criticism to
accommodate Christianity to the rationalism and antisupernaturalism
of the Newtonian worldview, denying the historicity of the biblical
references to the supernatural. Thus they explained away references to
*prophecy and *miracles on literary and textual grounds that followed
the example set by Paine in his *Age of Reason* (1794-1796). The impact
of biblical criticism on the rise of *new religions and the faith of the
founders of these religions cannot be underestimated. Once faith in the
authority of the Bible was lost, many began a quest for new forms of
religious faith based on nonbiblical sources.

biological racism. The nineteenth-century development of racism that
relates cultural differences to fundamental biological differences
among peoples. It was first advocated by the French author Count de
*Gobineau. Today it forms an important aspect of the beliefs of groups
like *Christian Identity.

biorhythms. A health fad of the 1970s *New Age movement that sought
to find links among human emotional changes, physical well-being
and a rhythmic cycle in nature based on a spiritual idea of *evolution.
The idea goes back to nineteenth-century physician Wilhelm Fliess,
whose work was popularized by George S. Thommen in various
books published in the late 1960s and 1970s. There seems to be no scientific basis for this view, and it is rapidly losing popularity through
its failure to help people cope with living. *See also* alternative medicine.

black mass. A blasphemous ritual enactment of the Roman Catholic
Mass used by Satanic groups. *See also* Satanism.

Black Muslims. An Islamic new religion or its members. This remarkably successful *new religious movement began as a bizarre cult and
developed into an orthodox branch of *Islam in North America. The
group was founded by Wallace D. *Fard around 1930 and originally
preached a race war against whites in which blacks would be aided by
spacemen. After Fard's disappearance in 1934, the group was led by
Elijah *Muhammad until his death, when several splinter groups
emerged. The principal outgrowth of this movement is now known as
the *Nation of Islam.

Blake, William (1757-1827). English poet and *mystic whose writings
inspired the *counterculture of the 1960s and movements such as *British Israelism.

Blavatsky, Helena Petrovna (1831-1891). Founder of the Theosophical Society. Born and educated in Russia, she appears to have led an adventurous life with numerous affairs before becoming a spiritualist in New York in the 1870s. She claimed to have visited Tibet and India, and she elaborated on the basic practices of *spiritualism by adding a rich, *eclectic mythology. Eventually she called her system *Theosophy and formed the *Theosophical Society in 1875. Her most important books are *Isis Unveiled* (1877) and *The Secret Doctrine* (three volumes, 1888-1897).

bodhisattva. A being who aspires to *enlightenment or Buddhahood. In the Mahayana Buddhist tradition the idea is developed to a point where the Bodhisattva becomes a savior figure who forgoes enlightenment to bring salvation to all sentient beings.

Böhme, Jakob (1575-1624). German Lutheran *mystic. Böhme's speculations about God and his relationship to creation drew upon Neo-Platonism, the Jewish *cabala and *alchemy and was expressed in his book *The Way to Christ* (1624). An obscure writer who was probably *orthodox in his actual beliefs, he has been accused of being both a *pantheist and a dualist. His work influenced Pietism, German *Romanticism and modern *New Age mystical movements as well as the writings of William Law (1686-1761) and Isaac Newton (1646-1727). His work was also appropriated by the *Nazis and various German *neopagan groups as a supreme example of the Germanic spirit and the value of *heretical thinking.

Bollingen Foundation. Research foundation. This exceptionally influential foundation was established in 1942 by Mary Mellon and her husband, Paul, to promote the works of Carl *Jung and an interest in ancient spirituality generally. (*See* Bollingen Series.) After spending millions of dollars to promote *occult topics, it was closed in 1969. It was closely linked to the *Eranos seminar. The story of the foundation is told in William McGuire's *Bollingen: An Adventure in Collecting the Past* (1982).

Bollingen Series. A highly influential series of books that includes the official translations of Carl G. *Jung's work. Most of the volumes in the Bollingen Series were produced with grants from the *Bollingen Foundation, which was primarily intended to promote Jung's ideas through the exploration of Eastern religions, *occult topics and ancient *mythology. Some of these works are highly scholarly, while others are more akin to *pseudoscience. Today the series is published by Princeton University Press and includes works such as *The Collected*

Works of C. G. Jung (1957-1979), *The Eranos Yearbooks* (1954-1968), Joseph *Campbell's *The Hero with a Thousand Faces* (1948), and Mircea *Eliade's *The Myth of the Eternal Return* (1954).

Book of Mormon. Mormon scripture. This collection of writings was published by Joseph *Smith in 1830. He claimed to have translated the book from some golden plates revealed to him by an *angel. The Book of Mormon tells the religious history of Native Americans and is essentially a Christian novel that is basically orthodox in its theology. Mormon doctrine departs from *orthodoxy through Joseph Smith's later revelations found in *Doctrine and Covenants.*

Book of the Dead. Magical texts. In Egyptian and Tibetan religious traditions a book of magical texts was placed in the grave alongside the corpse to secure blessing in the afterlife. Today the *Egyptian Book of the Dead* and *Tibetan Book of the Dead* are widely available in translations. They became popular in the *counterculture of the late 1960s and early 1970s that gave birth to many *new religions and the *New Age movement. *See also* Egyptian religions; magic; Tibetan Buddhism.

Brahma. The creator god in the Hindu tradition who is often associated with Vishnu and Siva. Brahma is not mentioned in the vedic hymns, where Prajapati is the creator god. Brahma is the masculine word for the neuter *Brahman, or "sacred power," which is ultimate reality. Although Vishnu and Siva are worshiped, there is no *cult of Brahma as an object of *bhakti, or devotion.

Brahman. A neutral term referring to the magical or sacred power implicit in the ritual sacrifices of vedic religion. It forms the basis of the word Brahmana, or *Brahmin, which refers to the priestly class that performed the sacred rituals. In some *Upanishads, Brahman is identified with the universe; in others, Brahman is regarded as a personal god or identified with *Atman (the eternal self within men). Within medieval Hindu theology, there were various disputes about the true nature of Brahman. The most important were between Sankara, who denied personal attributes, and *Ramanuja, who treated Brahman in a highly personalized manner.

Brahma-Sutra. The basic text of the *Vedanta tradition within the Hindu tradition. The work was probably composed in the second or third century A.D., but this is uncertain. Traditionally ascribed to Badaraya, the texts expound the *Upanishads. They were used extensively by Sankara, *Ramanuja and Madhava to develop their theologies and provide the basic *nondualism of modern Vedanta.

Brahmin. The priestly caste within Hindu society. Brahmin is the anglicized form of the *Sanskrit Brahmana—"one endowed with Brahman," or sacred power derived from sacrificial ritual. (*See* Brahman.) The Brahmins were traditionally the highest of the four varnas, or castes, of vedic society and retain high status even today.

Brahmo Samaj. Hindu reform movement. Founded by Ram Mohan *Roy in 1828, the movement developed a unitarian theology influenced by British utilitarianism and was strongly opposed to such things as temple cults, suttee (widow burning) and the caste system. The movement fostered Western education and sought to renew Indian society through European principles.

brainwashing. A term first used by an American journalist, Edward Hunter, in his book *Brain-washing in Red China* (1951) to describe techniques used by Chinese communists to overcome the resistance of their ideological opponents. *Brainwashing* was applied to religion as a theory explaining Christian conversion by London University psychiatrist William Sargent in his book *Battle for the Mind* (1957), written in the wake of the Billy Graham Crusade in London. Sargent concentrated on biblical accounts of conversion and the work of John Wesley (1703-1791), using the theories of the Russian psychiatrist Ivan Pavlov (1849-1936) to discredit religious experience. When the book first appeared, it was attacked by such prominent Christians as the physician-preacher Martyn Lloyd-Jones in *Conversions: Psychological and Spiritual* (1958) as "extremely dangerous." The term was popularized by Robert J. Lifton in his book *Thought Reform and the Psychology of Totalism* (1961), where he examined the application of psychological and physical pressure by Chinese communists to American prisoners of war for propaganda purposes during the Korean War. In the early 1970s the ideas of Lifton and Sargent were picked up by the American *anticult movement and popularized in such books as *Snapping* (1975) by Flo Conway and Jim Seigelman.

Branch Davidians. Apocalyptically oriented religious movement. This small movement traced its origins back to 1934 and claimed secret knowledge about the impending end of the world. (*See* apocalypticism.) Under the leadership of David *Koresh, the movement came to a fiery end in a tragic confrontation with American government forces at their compound in Waco, Texas, in April 1993.

Brandt, Johanna (1876-1964). Afrikaner *mystic whose books *The Millenium* (1918) and *Paraclete, or Coming World Mother* (1936) talked about such things as the coming *Age of Aquarius and feminist theology. Her books were resurrected in the 1960s and reissued in California, where they influenced the hippie movement.

breathing control. An essential aspect of *yoga and other *meditation practices within *yogic religions.

British Israelism. The idea that the English people are descendants of the "ten lost tribes" of Israel. This fringe form of *fundamentalism originated in the eighteenth century, and with its claim of descending from Israel it also maintains that it inherits all the biblical promises made to the Jewish people. In the twentieth century the most common form of this belief was found in its Americanized version preached by Herbert W. *Armstrong and the *Worldwide Church of God. The *Christian Identity movement grew out of British Israelism while shedding many of its more Christian and *apocalyptic beliefs.

Bromley, David (1941-). American sociologist. Bromley and Anson *Shupe are coauthors of *The Moonies in America* (1979) and *The New Vigilantes: Deprogramming, Anti-Cultists, and New Religions* (1980). These works gained them the enduring hatred of *anticult activists, who immediately labeled them *"cult apologists."

Buber, Martin (1878-1965). Jewish philosopher and theologian. Buber did much to bring about a Jewish intellectual renaissance in Central Europe in the 1920s. Influenced by Immanuel Kant (1724-1804), Friedrich *Nietzsche (1844-1900) and Søren Kierkegaard (1813-1855), Buber drew on the Jewish *Hasidic tradition with its doctrine that God is to be found in everything and everything in God and that the created world is to be redeemed rather than escaped from. His most famous work, the poem-essay *I and Thou* (1923-1937), influenced many Christian thinkers, including Paul Tillich (1886-1965) and Gabriel-Honoré Marcel (1889-1973). It also inspired many more unorthodox writers, particularly poets.

Buddhism. The Western name for what is generally known in Asia as the Buddha-Sasana, the religion or discipleship of the Buddha. Buddhism appears to have originated in northeast India in the sixth century B.C., and according to tradition was the outgrowth of the religious experience of Guatama, a young prince of the Sakya tribe. The doctrine he began to preach is known as the Dhamma (Dharma) and consists of an analysis of the human situation, existence and personality to provide a means of transcending suffering and mortality, and achieving a new state of being. The following that grew around the Buddha was regarded by contemporary Hindu priests (Brahman) as heretical; the Buddha is often represented as engaging in controversy with Brahmans. Numerous schools of Buddhist thought developed over the centuries.

Modern groups such as the Tendai, Zen and Pure Land schools grew out of the Mahayan tradition, which in turn grew out of an earlier movement taking a liberal interpretation of Buddhist monastic disciplines.

C

cabala (kabalah, qabalah). Medieval Jewish mystical system. (*See* mysticism.) Cabala is based on the Bible but draws on Platonism and a variety of other philosophical traditions. The major written source is known as the *Zohar*.

Caddy, Eileen (1917-). English *occultist. Eileen Caddy was Egyptian-born and the first wife of Peter *Caddy. In 1953 she had a mystical experience in *Glastonbury, England, that led her to become a channeler, or spiritualist medium. In 1957 she helped establish the *Findhorn Community, which she continued to lead for many years. Claiming to be in communication with *nature spirits, such as the god Pan, she is also important as a leader of the *neopagan movement.

Caddy, Peter (1917-1994). English *occultist, strongly influenced by *theosophy, who cofounded the *Findhorn Community in the mid-1960s. He later divorced his wife, Eileen, who had acted as his medium, and moved to Mount Shasta, California, where he founded the Gathering of the Ways Center, modeled after Findhorn.

Campbell, Alexander (1788-1866). Founder of the Disciples of Christ. Born and educated in Ireland, Campbell immigrated to the United States in 1809 and spent several years as an itinerant preacher. His teachings—found in his magazines *The Christian Baptist* (1823-1830) and *The Millennial Harbinger* (1830-1866) and books like *The Christian System* (1839)—gave birth to groups of believers known as Campbellites or as Disciples of Christ. The Disciples of Christ later joined with Barton Stone's churches to form the Christian Church (Disciples of Christ). Although Campbell's movement was orthodox, his teachings on the end times eventually had a profound influence on unorthodox groups like the *Christadelphians and *Jehovah's Witnesses.

Campbell, Joseph (1904-1987). American *occultist and college professor. Campbell's prolific but confused ideas about mythology made him a cult figure for the *counterculture of the 1960s and later the *New Age movement. Campbell was influenced by *traditionalist thinkers like René *Guénon, Julius *Evola, Frithjof *Schuon and Ananda *Coomaraswamy, through whom he gained his academic position after dropping out of graduate school. But his views were essentially fascist, drawing on ideas of *myth that are to be found in the writings of Alfred *Rosenberg.

Capra, Fritjof (1931-). American physicist and New Age thinker. Capra is author of the bestselling *Tao of Physics* (1975). He became a *New Age guru because of his speculations about the relationship between modern physics and *yogic religions.

cargo cult. A type of *new religious movement involving a hope for wealth. The term originates from the anthropological study of Polynesian culture, where the followers of a *prophet figure are promised the arrival of "cargo" brought by a savior figure on magical airplanes. This figure would free the people from oppression and usher in a new order. The term is now commonly applied to all new religions where the promise of earthly prosperity seems to be a major factor in making converts.

Castaneda, Carlos (1935-1998). Author of *The Teachings of Don Juan: A Yanqui Way of Knowledge* (1968) and a number of other books purporting to be anthropological accounts of a Native American *shamanistic religious tradition. Although Castaneda was awarded a Ph.D. in 1973 by the University of California for his work, many scholars doubt the authenticity of his studies and question the appropriateness of his being awarded a doctorate. His books were popular and his teachings contributed to the growth of *counterculture spirituality and interest in *esoteric religion.

Catholic Apostolic Church. Christian denomination. Sometimes known as the "Irvingites," this group was founded by Edward *Irving and originated as a charismatic group but soon developed liturgical aspects similar to Roman Catholicism and Greek Orthodoxy but with a strong emphasis on the imminent return of Christ. As a movement, it had some success in the late nineteenth century before entering a period of slow decline. Today its influence is felt mostly among *new religious movements in the Third World, especially in Africa.

Cayce, Edgar (1877-1945). American psychic. Cayce's writings provided much of the impetus for channeling in the *New Age movement as well as promoting belief in *yogic religion and such things as *reincarnation. After experiencing healing as the result of a trance, he gradually became a popular psychic reader and lecturer. In 1931 Cayce founded the Association for Research and Enlightenment and began issuing regular newsletters. After his death, his son turned his writings into a series of popular books that gained a wide following.

CESNUR. Centre for Studies on New Religions. CESNUR was founded in 1988 by Italian lawyer Massimo Introvigne. The group maintains an extensive website and has formed branches in other European countries and North America. CESNUR, which runs a research library in Torino, Italy, has created a network of scholars who attempt to promote understanding by providing members, reporters and legislators with reliable information about new religions. Critics of the group claim that it is a procult front and attempt to link it to controversial new religions like *Scientology. Such charges appear to be totally unfounded and an exercise in guilt by association. Actually, most of the founding members were committed Roman Catholics, although its membership now includes scholars from other religious groups and even some who profess no religious affiliation. The website contains extensive documentation and is regularly updated, making it a valuable source for information on new religions. The group also publishes a highly informative Internet newsletter.

Chamberlain, Houston Stewart (1855-1927). Prophet of Germanic religion. Born in England, Chamberlain was the son-in-law of German composer Richard *Wagner. Chamberlain's *Foundations of the Nineteenth Century* (1900) was a bestseller in both England and Germany. He argued for a form of religion similar to that found in *Christian Identity and related movements that was based on race theory and the rejection of traditional theology because of the findings of *biblical criticism.

channeling. *See* trance channeling.

charisma. From the Greek word meaning "favor" or "grace." It was used by the sociologist Max *Weber to describe the attraction of a person with a magnetic personality or great gifts of leadership such as those found in Alexander the Great or Napoleon. Weber then applied this idea to religious leaders as a means of explaining the appeal of people like the Buddha, Moses, Jesus, Paul and Muhammad. In this way it came to refer to the personal magnetism of leaders who are able to attract a devoted following. In popular Christianity *charisma* refers to the gifts of the Spirit that are believed to follow the baptism of the Holy Spirit. Such gifts include healing, prophecy and speaking in tongues.

Children of God. A *new religious movement originating in the late 1960s and subsequently called the Family of Love. Children of God began as part of the Jesus movement in California and was founded by David *Berg, who became known as Moses David, or "Mo." Developing charismatic gifts, the group then began to encourage *prophecy. This practice led to various *occult activities and a form of *spiritualism through the invocation of spiritual guides such as "the Pied Piper," who Mo claimed communicated with him. Mo prophesied the imminent destruction of California and the whole American system and told his followers to disperse throughout the world. Espousing what it called "godly socialism," the group's main theological reference became the *Mo Letters.* Children of God was one of the first *new religious movements to receive the attention of the *anticult movement, and its activities led directly to the development of deprogramming by Ted Patrick. One of the most highly publicized practices of the group was the use of "flirty fishing," which involved prostitution as a conversion technique. Today it is an essentially underground movement with an estimated 2,000 members worldwide.

chiliasm. Term for millennial belief, taken from the Greek word meaning "one thousand." Speculation about the importance of a millennium occur in many religions traditions, such as Zoroastrianism, as well as in Greek philosophers, such as *Plato. In Christianity millennial beliefs have taken various forms, especially premillennialism, which looks for the imminent return of Christ prior to the inauguration of the millennium. *See also* apocalypse; apocalypticism; millenarian movements; millennialism.

Christadelphians. An American *sect. The Christadelphians were founded in 1848 by John Thomas (1805-1871), who believed in the imminent return of Christ, denied Christ's divinity and rejected the Trinity. In many ways this group is similar to the *Jehovah's Witnesses, who were influenced by Thomas's teachings.

Christian Identity. White racist movement. This diverse pseudoreligious movement originated in the 1940s as an American development of *British Israelism infused with *occult ideas and *millenarian beliefs derived from *pyramidology. Despite its name, the group is essentially a white racist movement with a worldview that is remarkably similar to that of Alfred *Rosenberg. The leading authority on the group, Michael Barkun, says that, contrary to what is commonly believed, the movement has nothing to do with, and is actually hostile to, Christian *fundamentalism. (See Michael Barkun, *Christian Identity* [1999].)

Christian Research Institute. Christian apologetic organization. The institute was founded in 1960 by Walter *Martin, a Baptist minister who was concerned about the growth of groups like the *Jehovah's Witnesses and *Mormons. The Christian Research Institute was the first major evangelical Christian organization to specialize in combating new religions. Following Martin's death, the leadership of the organization was assumed by Hank H. Hanegraaff, a prolific author and conference speaker who continues the tradition of *countercult apologetics originated by Martin.

Christian Science. A religion founded by Mary Baker *Eddy. Eddy believed she had been healed after a severe injury in 1866. She then dedicated her life to promoting a form of healing based on ideas taken from Christianity, Hinduism and Buddhism. In 1875 her book *Science and Health with Key to the Scriptures* was published, and on August 23, 1879, the Church of Christ, Scientist, was incorporated in Boston, Massachusetts. Christian Science teaches a synthesis of *Abramic and *yogic religions on the premise that God is the "Divine Principle of all that really is."

church. The word *church* is used in various senses. In the New Testament the Greek word *ekklēsia* (translated in English as *church*) designates the community created by the preaching of the gospel of Jesus Christ. In Christian theology church members are those people who participate in baptism, receive the gift of the Holy Spirit and gather together for common worship and the celebration of Holy Communion. Sociologically, *church* is used to refer to a religious organization that is universal in its scope. According to the sociologists Max *Weber and Ernst Troeltsch, a church is any religious organization that is universal in its scope and inclusive in membership. That is, a church is a religious body that counts as its members anyone living within a certain geographic area. Sociologists Rodney *Stark and William Sims Bainbridge define a church as a conventional religious organization.

Church of Christ, Scientist. *See* Christian Science.

Churchward, James (1832-1936). Theosophical writer. (*See* Theosophy.) Churchward wrote a number of books about a long-lost continent called *Mu, which he said had an advanced civilization and was located in the Pacific region. He claimed to have made his discovery through the study of ancient art, history, *mythology and the *occult. Churchward was influenced by Ignatius *Donnelly, Helena *Blavatsky and Ernst *Haeckel.

civil religion. The general faith of a state that reflects widely held beliefs about the history or destiny of the state. This idea, developed by Jean Jacques Rousseau (1712-1778) in *The Social Contract* (1762), was taken up by American sociologist Robert Bellah to explain the development of religion in America. In Bellah's usage civil religion is a vague religious sentiment promoted by state institutions on the basis of common ideas held by all citizens, and as such it avoids dogma (such as belief in Christ) and emphasizes an undefined belief in God and providence.

Coleridge, Samuel Taylor (1772-1834). English poet, critic and philosopher. Coleridge's early rationalism gave way to a mystical religion influenced by Jakob *Böhme and Baruch Spinoza. He preached against orthodox Protestantism in favor of a spiritualized religiosity unhampered by the constraints of biblical *revelation. *See also* mysticism.

Comte, Auguste (1798-1857). French positivist philosopher and one of the founders of sociology. Comte sought to create a new *scientific religion. His major work is *The System of Positive Policy* (four volumes, 1851-1854).

Confucianism. The major Chinese philosophical, political and social tradition based on the teachings of Confucius (551-479 B.C.). The main idea of the tradition is the Tao, or Way to Heaven, which is to be practiced by all people and emphasizes loyalty and the cultivation of humanity. According to Confucius, inner goodness finds expression in outward behavior. His writings were compiled as *The Analects of Confucius.*

Conze, Edward (1904-1979). Buddhist scholar. Conze was an English-born German communist who fled Nazi Germany to take refuge in England in 1933. He converted to Buddhism and became the greatest twentieth-century interpreter of Buddhism to the West. His book *Buddhism: Its Essence and Development* (1951) is the best single introduction to Buddhism, while his *Buddhist Thought in India* (1962) remains an undervalued classic. His autobiography, *The Memoirs of a Modern Gnostic* (1979), is entertaining reading for anyone wishing to understand modern religious thought.

Coomaraswamy, Ananda Kentish (1877-1947). Art historian and traditionalist. Coomaraswamy was the son of an English mother and a Ceylonese father, Sir Mutu Coomaraswamy, who died while his son was a child. He was educated in England, where he studied geology at the University of London before taking a post in the Department of Mines in Ceylon (now Sri Lanka). In 1917 he emigrated to America, where he became the curator at the Boston Museum of Fine Arts. Although never formally educated in art history, he wrote many books on the subject, some of which became standard texts on Asian art. He was strongly influenced by the writings of Helena *Blavatsky and later became a close friend and colleague of René *Guénon, with whom he helped create the *traditionalist school of thinkers. Coomaraswamy

hated the modern world and blamed Christian missionaries for
spreading *modernity to Asia. His political views are indistinguish-
able from intellectual *fascism, although unlike some of his fellow traditionalists, he never openly identified with fascist thinking. He
worked closely with Mary Mellon (d. 1946), Heinrich Zimmer (1890-
1943) and the *Bollingen Foundation, through which he was a creative
influence on such people as Mircea *Eliade and Joseph *Campbell and
later Huston *Smith, Jacob *Needleman and Ken *Wilber. His books
include *Christian and Oriental Philosophy of Art* (1974), *Buddha and the
Gospel of Buddhism* (1988) and *What Is Civilization?* (1989).

countercult. A term popularized by researchers like Douglas Cowan to
distinguish between Christian organizations that seek to combat new
religions on the basis of theological critiques and groups like the
*American Family Foundation that attack new religions on the basis of
psychological and other kinds of damage they supposedly do to members and society. (*See* anticult movement.) *Countercult* is used to identify those critics of new religions, or cults, who concentrate on
theological issues and on the differences between such groups and
Christian *orthodoxy. *See also* cult; new religious movements.

counterculture. The social movement that emerged in the Haight-Ash-
bury district of San Francisco in 1967 in connection with the hippies.
The counterculture movement was a social protest against Western
cultural values and a spiritual search for alternate realities at first
through the use of hallucinogenic drugs and later through *yogic religions. The counterculture paved the way for the *New Age movement
and is best summarized in *The Making of a Counter-Culture* (1970) by
Theodore Roszak.

Course in Miracles, A. A self-study spiritual thought course. The book
A Course in Miracles was written as a result of strange dreams experienced by Helen *Schucman (1909-1981), who said she heard the voice
of Jesus. The teaching of the course combines *theosophical ideas,
*positive thinking and Christian terminology. The book has sold al-
most two million copies.

Culdees. Irish and Scottish monks, originating in the eighth century,
who usually lived in groups of thirteen. In the nineteenth century they
became the subject of *neopagan speculation and were erroneously
linked to the *druids. This usage has passed into various *new religious movements as a way of seeking to establish legitimacy for *esoteric beliefs.

cult. A controversial and misunderstood word greatly misused by the media, where it is applied to groups nobody likes and is associated with *brainwashing. In theology the term *cult* has been used to refer to forms of worship and the rituals associated with them, such as those at the Jerusalem temple in ancient Judaism. Sociologically, it refers to small religious groups that are in tension with established religious traditions and society generally. In their book *A Theory of Religion* (1987) Rodney *Stark and William Sims Bainbridge give an operational definition of a cult as "a religious body which does not have a prior tie with another established religious body in the society in question. The cult may represent an alien (external) religion, or it may have originated in the host society, but through innovation, not fusion. Whether domestic or imported, the cult is something new *vis-à-vis* the other religious bodies in the society in question" (p. 124). On the basis of this definition, they identify three types of cults: (1) "Audience cults" resemble a lecture circuit where people participate in lectures, seminars and workshops as well as buy books and subscribe to magazines that promote a spiritual point of view. (2) "Client cults" are those groups in which mobilization is partial, rather than all-embracing, and in which people participate as clients (for example, by attending occasional spiritualist meetings) when they have specific needs, rather than join as members. (3) "Cult movements" proper are those movements in which membership is required and there is a development toward the status of a *sect. (*See* audience cults; cult movements.) More generally, a cult is a deviant religious organization with novel beliefs and practices.

cult apologist. A term of abuse used to discredit scholars who reject the argument that conversion to new religions is the result of *brainwashing and whose work is seen by members of the *anticult movement as dangerous. Instead of criticizing on scholarly grounds the work of people like Eileen *Barker, David *Bromley, Jeffrey *Hadden, Gordon *Melton and Anson *Shupe, the preferred tactic of anticult activists is to launch vicious ad hominem attacks, usually involving the false allegation that they are in the pay of specific cults such as *Scientology and the *Unification Church. The fact that these are all distinguished scholars who have reached their conclusions on the basis of extensive scientific research is totally ignored by their critics, most of whom lack university education. *See also* cult; new religious movements.

cult movements. Rodney *Stark's term for new religions that form definite organizations with an identifiable membership. *See also* cult.

D

Daishi, Dengyo (766-822). Buddhist innovator, also known as Saicho. He introduced to Japan the Buddhist *sect of *Tendai, which gave birth to *Nichiren Buddhism and in modern times to various *new religions.

Daishi, Kobo (774-835). The posthumous name of Kukai, a Japanese Buddhist saint and founder of *Shingon, an *esoteric form of Buddhism. After studying in China, he introduced *tantric practices and *pantheistic *mystical ideas into Japanese Buddhism in a *syncretistic manner that influenced the development of *Shinto.

Dalai Lama. The title given to the head of the Yellow School of Monks in *Tibetan Buddhism and a popular figure among many contemporary *occult groups.

Däniken, Erich von (1935-). Influential Swiss writer who runs his own theme park in Switzerland. He rose to fame as a result of his bestselling *Chariots of the Gods* (1968), which suggested that ancient civilizations were visited by space aliens who assisted in their creation and achievements. This book (like his subsequent books—twenty-five in all) was written as a scientific detective story in which von Däniken appears to piece together ancient evidence that he claims are mysteries in terms of conventional archaeology. In fact, most of the "mysteries" are his own invention and, as critics point out, his "evidence" does not stand up to expert examination. In reality von Däniken secularized the arguments of George *Adamski by removing his explicit *theosophical references to make them acceptable to a new generation. Many *New Age writers, including Shirley *Maclaine, owe him an immense debt.

Darwin, Charles Robert (1809-1882). English scientist and evolutionary thinker. Darwin is remembered for his seminal work, *The Origin of Species* (1859), which purported to provide strong empirical evidence for the theory of *evolution. Darwin's views were shaped by his own observations while aboard the HMS *Beagle,* where he worked as a naturalist, and from his reading of both the theologian William Paley (1743-1805) and the geologist Charles Lyell (1797-1875). Following the publication of *Origin,* Darwin was engaged in continuous controversy because, although he appears to have remained a theist, his views were seen as a frontal attack on Christian belief. Later, Helene *Blavatsky and numerous other founders of new religions merged a popular understanding of Darwinism with ideas of spiritual evolution and *yogic religions.

Dead Sea Scrolls. A collection of early Jewish manuscripts discovered in 1948 in several caves at *Qumran, near the Dead Sea. In addition to Old Testament texts, the scrolls contain numerous other documents relating to the rituals, discipline and beliefs of an unnamed Jewish *sect often identified as *Essenes. In the popular press, controversy has surrounded the interpretation of this material, which has now entered the world of *occult and *new religious movements as a source of inspiration. The texts are often wrongly identified with *Gnostic traditions by modern spiritual writers who are ignorant of the true nature of the scrolls.

deification. The making of a person or thing into a deity. Deification is characteristic of many *pagan religions and often involves the elevation of heroes to the rank of gods. In Eastern Orthodox theology the term has a technical meaning similar to sanctification in Western theology. That is, through the work of the Holy Spirit, humans are believed to regain those attributes belonging to the likeness of God lost at the Fall. Orthodox theologians are careful to point out that this process is to be clearly distinguished from the blurring of the distinction between the creature and Creator, as found in *pagan religions and more recently in the type of *New Age writing represented by people like Shirley *Maclaine.

deism. A philosophy that regards God as the intelligent Creator of an independent and law-abiding world but denies that he providentially guides it or intervenes in any way with its course or destiny. For the deist, reason is the sole instrument through which God's existence and nature can be deduced from the orderly workings of the universe. Deism flourished in England in the eighteenth century and strongly influenced the rise of *biblical criticism and *modernism in the nineteenth century. In North America it is associated with views of Benjamin Franklin (1706-1790), Thomas Jefferson (1743-1826) and, most of all, Thomas *Paine (1737-1809), where it often merged with a religion of nature. Deism entered German universities through the University of Göttingen, where the English influence was strong, and influenced people such as Ludwig *Feuerbach (1804-1872).

demons. Evil spirits who seek to harm humans. *See also* angels; exorcism.

deprivation theory. A popular sociological theory, inspired by Marxism, that religious movements can be explained in terms of the poverty ("deprivation") of their members.

deprogramming. A practice developed by Ted *Patrick (b. 1930) based on the assumption that religious conversion involves "brainwashing." Many deprogrammers began in the 1970s and 1980s to "rescue" people from "cults" through techniques that usually involved kidnapping and involuntary detention. Eventually the cruder aspects of deprogramming were outlawed and dropped from widespread use. The theory that "cult members" are brainwashed is based on the work of English psychiatrist William *Sargant, whose book *Battle for the Mind* (1957) applied theories of brainwashing developed during the Korean war to Christian conversion—particularly the work of Billy Graham. Flo Conway and Jim Siegelman applied the theories to new religions and cults in their book *Snapping* (1978) and to evangelical Christians in *Holy Terror* (1982).

dharma. Literally, that which is established law, the wheel of existence, ultimate truth. *Dharma* is a term used by Buddhists, Hindus and *Jains to describe the human situation and the way or means of salvation. It is a complex concept that is often misunderstood and needs to be seen in the context of Indian religious and philosophical thought. Among other things, *dharma* implies a moral order expressed through the network of human rights and obligations supported by a cosmic universal order and the caste system.

dianetics. A theory, book and therapy developed by L. Ron *Hubbard, the founder of *Scientology. Hubbard taught that psychological and other problems result from "engrams," or bad impressions, in the subconscious mind. Negative engrams must be eliminated to enable individuals to realize their natural and spiritual potential.

dispensationalism. A type of biblical interpretation found among *fundamentalist and conservative evangelical Christians that finds God's dealings with humans divided into "times" or "dispensations" characterized by unique opportunities and responsibilities. This view originally characterized the Plymouth Brethren and was popularized in the *Scofield Reference Bible* (1910). Many *new religious movements, such as the *Unification Church, are strongly influenced by dispensationalism, which they adapt to their own ends.

divination. The foretelling of the future using such means as *astrology, augury and auspices. In principle the future course of events is read from patterns found in the stars, the entrails of animals and such things as the way bones or sticks fall when thrown. Divination plays an important role in many religious systems and is central to many *folk religions.

Divine Light Mission. A modern Hindu missionary movement. The movement was founded by Shri Hans Maharaj Ji (d. 1966) and came to the West in 1971 under the leadership of his son, the then thirteen-year-old guru Maharaj Ji (b. 1959). After initial success and extensive media coverage, the movement floundered due to mounting debts and internal strife. The movement is an offshoot of the Sant Mat, a *Sikh *sect strongly influenced by Hinduism.

Doctrine and Covenants. A series of revelations published by Joseph *Smith in 1835. In these revelations Smith claims to be a *prophet with a unique message from God, and it is here that Smith's theology radically departs from traditional Christianity. The book is regarded as scripture by *Mormons.

Donnelly, Ignatius T. T. (1831-1901). Philadelphia populist politician and author of *The Antediluvian World* (1882). Donnelly popularized the idea of *Atlantis as a "lost continent" and home of an ancient race from which both the Egyptian and Mayan civilizations sprang. His ideas were adopted and incorporated into the writings by Helena *Blavatsky, who gave them a spiritual twist.

Drucker, Peter F. (1909-). Austrian-American thinker sometimes called the father of modern management. His first English book, *The End of Economic Man* (1939), is a brilliant analysis of the intellectual, moral and social crisis facing the *modern world.

druids. An ancient *pagan religious priesthood found in Celtic lands, including Britain and areas of France. The Romans totally destroyed druidism, with the result that our only knowledge of it comes from Roman sources that describe it as entailing a bloody system of human sacrifice. Since the eighteenth century, various new religious groups have claimed to be druids, but there is no historical evidence that any of them are remotely related to ancient druidism. Today many "druid" groups seek to perform their rituals at *Stonehenge, which was a ruin long before the Celts entered Britain and has no connection with ancient druidism.

Dukhobors. Communal sect, whose name literally means "spirit wrestlers." This Russian religious *sect, founded in the eighteenth century, is characterized by a rejection of civic authority and a tendency toward communalism. Persecuted during the nineteenth century, the Dukhobors emigrated to Canada, where small communities still exist. Some branches of the Dukhobors are *orthodox Christians in their theological beliefs, while others are *heretical.

Dukkha (Pali), Duhkha (Sanskrit). One of the three characteristic marks of existence in Buddhism. It is usually translated "suffering," but this should be understood as a radical suffering that characterizes the whole of existence.

E

Eckankar. A *new religious movement professing to be based on ancient wisdom. Eckankar was founded in 1965 by Paul Twitchell (1908-1971), who popularized his ideas through his books *The Tiger's Fang* (1967) and *Eckankar* (1969). Also influential was Brad Steiger's biography, *In My Soul I Am Free* (1968). Twitchell claimed to be the 971st ECK master and to be revealing a long-secret tradition to the modern world. His teachings include *reincarnation, soul travel and a variety of *yogic and *occult beliefs and practices. After Twitchell's death, he was succeeded by Darwin Gross as the 972nd ECK master. Gross married Twitchell's widow, but following their divorce in 1978 the group split, and Gross was succeeded by Harold Klemp, who became the 973rd ECK master. Eckankar is an offshoot of Kirpal Singh's Ruhani Satsang and the Self-Revelation Church and owes many of its ideas to the Indian Sant Mat tradition.

eclectic. An adjective describing ideas and practices that have been taken from different traditions and arbitrarily joined together as though they belong to a unified system. The term is used in religious studies and philosophy to describe people and systems that borrow widely without any real unified structure.

ecstasy. Literally, "standing outside oneself." This term is often applied to those psychic or spiritual states that are supposed to seize *mystics and *prophets.

Eddy, Mary Baker (1821-1910). Founder of the Church of Christ, Scientist (popularly known as *Christian Science) and author of *Science and Health with Key to the Scriptures* (1875). Eddy was a physically weak woman, but her teachings arose after she experienced a profound physical healing, which she attributed to the work of God. Her teachings consist of a Christianized form of *Hinduism that draws inspiration from many other religious and metaphysical sources. Probably her most lasting achievement outside her church was the establishment of *The Christian Science Monitor*, a world-class newspaper with recognized high standards of journalism.

egoism. The belief that all actions are performed out of self-interest. Ayn *Rand and others have developed this viewpoint into a systematic theory that all actions *ought* to be performed out of self-interest. Tradition-

ally the great world religions have condemned egoism as either sinful
or undesirable. Many *new religions, such as *Scientology, promote
views that appear similar to those of Rand.

Egyptian religions. Long-dead religious traditions known from ancient
texts and archaeological reports that now form the basis for worship
among several small groups of *neopagans.

eightfold path. Buddhist exposition of the means by which a believer
may gain *enlightenment. Although not found in the earliest Buddhist
texts, the eightfold path is generally accepted as a basic tenet of Buddhism and is usually divided into three areas: faith, morality and
*meditation. The eightfold path consists of (1) "right understanding";
(2) "right thought," which refers to faith; (3) "right speech"; (4) "right
bodily action"; (5) "right livelihood," which refers to morality; (6)
"right effort"; (7) "right mindfulness"; and (8) "right concentration,"
which refers to *meditation. It is thus a systematic summary of Buddhist belief that may be expanded into much longer treatises.

Einstein, Albert (1879-1955). Mathematician and physicist. An immigrant to America from Germany, Einstein's work radically changed
our ideas about space and time. Together with Max Planck's quantum
theory, Einstein's work on relativity laid the foundations for modern
physics. Popular misunderstandings of his work have promoted the
idea that everything—morals, truth and so on—is relative and have
helped boost religious developments like the *New Age movement.

Eleusinian mysteries. Ancient mystery religion. Information about
these rites, which took place as part of a mystery religion at Eleusis
near Athens, is fragmentary and unreliable. Initiation lasted two years
and involved vows of secrecy. The cult was suppressed in the fourth
century A.D. Today various *occult groups claim that their practices
were inspired by the Eleusinian mysteries, although in reality no historical link can be established.

Eliade, Mircea (1907-1988). Historian of religion. Eliade's original ambi-
tion was to be a novelist. An emigrant from Romania, Eliade became
professor of religious studies at the University of Chicago in 1956.
From there he exercised a vast influence on the development of religious studies. His work reflects an interest in a highly mythical and ab-
stract spirituality that has been strongly criticized by anthropologists
and historians for its detachment from empirical reality. Of his book
Shamanism, the Buddhist scholar Edward *Conze wrote, "[It] is probably the best we have on the subject. The more one reads it the more un-
convincing it becomes." Conze further claimed that every time he

checked a citation from Eliade's *Yoga, Immortality and Freedom* (1936) against an original text, he discovered that it was a misquote. The *Bollingen Foundation helped Eliade establish himself in North America by supporting his research for books such as *The Myth of the Eternal Return* (1954). Adriana Berger claims that Eliade was not only a *fascist but also a German spy. Naturally, Berger's work has been discounted by Eliade's students. Nevertheless, there is independent evidence that Eliade visited various *Nazi thinkers while touring Germany in the 1930s, although references to these visits were deleted from his published diaries. Further, Eliade had contact with Jakob Wilhelm *Hauer, the creator of the pro-Nazi *Glaubensbewegung* (German Faith Movement), as early as 1928. In themselves these contacts prove nothing, although they may explain the fact that the structure of Eliade's ideas about religion reflect those of Hauer while his views on *myth are almost identical to those of various German Nazi thinkers, including Alfred *Rosenberg.

emanationism. The view that the universe flows from the being of God like rays shine forth from the sun. This viewpoint is found in *yogic philosophies and such Western systems as Neo-Platonism and *Gnosticism.

emergent evolution. The idea that life and consciousness emerged out of inert matter and will ultimately evolve to a godlike state. This theory finds expression in the philosophy of Henri *Bergson. *See also* evolution.

Emerson, Ralph Waldo (1803-1882). American essayist and leader of the Transcendentalist movement. Emerson was minister of the *Unitarian Second Church of Boston (1829-1832) but resigned over theological issues to become an independent lecturer and writer. His philosophy drew on *yogic religions to combine rationalism and *mysticism. He also encouraged a strong emphasis on self-reliance and a belief in the ability of the individual to overcome all problems. Although much more profound than they, he was the forerunner of Dale Carnegie and other *"positive thinkers" who have been influential in shaping popular piety in America. And although Emerson's own writings are essentially secular, his influence can be seen in the so-called *New Age movement and a host of other popular spiritual movements seeking inner truth.

enlightenment. The attainment of an exalted state of spiritual knowledge, awareness or bliss in *yogic religions. In Buddhism it is the revelatory experience of the Buddha and the attainment of *nirvana.

Enlightenment, the. A philosophical movement characterized by the historian Ernst Troeltsch (1865-1923) as the beginning of the truly *modern period of European culture. It had its roots in Protestant Christianity, was strongly influenced by Pietism and was welcomed by many Christians, including John Wesley (1703-1791), who sought to promote a form of Christian Enlightenment that advanced the cause of religious and social freedom. The Enlightenment proper found its clearest expression in the work of Immanuel Kant (1724-1804), who defined the Enlightenment, in his book *Religion Within the Limits of Reason* (1793), as humanity's emergence from a self-inflicted state of minority. Kant wrote, "Have the courage to make use of your own understanding, is therefore the watchword of the Enlightenment." The Enlightenment originated in Calvinist circles in the Netherlands, England and Scotland in the mid-seventeenth century, but it reached its high-water mark in French rationalism and materialism, finding political expression in the French Revolution. Its richest philosophical and political results were achieved in Germany under the influence of Kant. Although many branches of the Enlightenment were self-consciously anti-Christian, a distinctive form of rationalistic Enlightenment Christianity developed in some Protestant countries. Other branches of Protestantism, such as Methodism, combined the social concerns of Enlightenment thinkers with a love of reason and a strong biblical faith. The historian Peter Gay and others have also pointed out that, while the Enlightenment is usually remembered as a movement of reason, there was a strong *occult undercurrent, leading him to describe the movement in terms of the "birth of modern paganism."

Enquete-Kommission. A German government commission of inquiry into *new religious movements. It was set up in 1997, under the instigation of people such as Thomas *Gandow, to investigate "so-called sects, cults and psycho-groups." The commission's final report, issued in 1999, argued that while most new religions are harmless, some might be dangerous. Therefore the government ought to fund the training of *anticult workers and create exit programs to help people leave new religions. More recently similar commissions have been established in France and several other European countries.

Enroth, Ronald M. (1938-). One of the first contemporary Christians to address the issue of new religions, which he did in the 1970s. His book *Youth Religions and Destructive Cults* (1977) set the tone for many evangelical *countercult arguments.

Eranos Seminar. Seminar on religion. The name Eranos (suggested to the seminar's founder, Olga *Froebe, by Rudolf *Otto) is based on a Greek word meaning a "shared feast." This elite seminar and series of lectures, established in 1933, was dominated by Carl *Jung until his death in 1961. A list of participants in the seminar reads like a Who's Who of Religious Studies. Prominent participants include Heinrich Zimmer (1890-1943), Mircea *Eliade (1907-1988) and many others. Although many of its early members were actually persecuted by the *Nazis, they often shared a common set of values and interests that can be identified as *völkish thought. The conferences, which continue to the present, are a major channel for the propagation of *occult and *New Age-type thought among intellectuals. Previously they were closely linked to the *Bollingen Foundation and its series of books. (See Steven M. Wasserstrom, *Religion After Religion* [1999].) This group should not be confused with the Swedish philosophical journal of the same name.

Erhard Seminar Training. *See* EST.

Erhard, Werner (1935-). Founder of *EST. Born Jack Rosenberg, he is an *occultist who in 1971 founded EST, an *eclectic type of self-development and spiritual technique based largely on ideas and practices derived from *Zen Buddhism and *Scientology.

eschatology. Literally, "discourse about the last things." It refers to that aspect of a religion that deals with the final end of the world and humankind. *See also* apocalypse.

esoteric. From the Greek term meaning "inner" or "hidden." Today it refers to secret teachings that either belong to secret societies or lie behind the official beliefs that a religious group proclaims to the world. Many *new religious movements are based on claims that they, and they alone, know the "true" meaning of a religious teacher's message and that the apparent teaching conceals its real meaning.

ESP. Extrasensory perception, or claims by individuals to experience paranormal phenomena such as telepathy, *prophecies, significant or prophetic dreams, visions and powers to levitate and affect physical objects by mental power. Although most claims of this nature clearly belong to the realm of *pseudoscience, sufficient examples exist in the experience of many people to leave open the possibility that some powers of this nature do exist. But in general there are two problems with such claims: (1) they clearly violate the known laws of modern science; and (2) they are often made in connection with bizarre theories derived from *yogic religions and *spiritualism and are devoid of any rational justification.

Essenes. Ancient Jewish *sect. From ancient writers (Josephus, Philo, Pliny) we learn that the Essenes lived in cities of Palestine as well as in a monastic-like community in the vicinity of the Dead Sea. Some of their beliefs and practices are known, but much speculation surrounds them. They are generally believed to be the group whose "library" was discovered at *Qumran and is known as the *Dead Sea Scrolls (although some scholars question this assumption). Since the nineteenth century, various *esoteric religious movements have claimed continuity with the Essenes and used their name to propagate their own views. Such groups must be recognized as *new religious movements lacking historical justifications for their claims, which are no more than wild speculations.

EST. Erhard Seminar Training, a program involving spiritual practices derived from *Zen Buddhism and *Scientology. Founded in 1971 by Werner *Erhard, the movement (which has operated under a variety of names), organizes intense weekend seminars intended to break down inhibitions and put the individual in touch with his or her true self. Many participants report *occult experiences and encounters with spirit beings toward the end of the seminar, which is officially nonreligious. Generally EST has helped promote a type of self-enlightenment and has fostered views that, in turn, have helped promote the *New Age movement.

establishment/disestablishment. Terms describing the relationship between a church and a state. When a church is "established," it is the official religion of a country and is supported by law and given special privileges in exchange for varying amounts of government control. Disestablishment means the removal of special status from churches by the state. Many European churches are established churches. American churches are "free" or "disestablished." In Europe many groups regarded as churches or denominations in North America and Britain are seen as *cults or *sects simply because they are not the established church of a region or country.

eternal progression. The *Mormon doctrine that theorizes a spiritual *evolution for humanity resulting in *deification. The idea was summed up by the Mormon apostle Lorenzo Snow (1814-1901), who said, "As man is, God was. As God is, man may become."

eternal recurrence. The idea that time is cyclical and all events ultimately repeat themselves. This belief merges with ideas of reincarnation to explain the history of the world and to support ideas like soul travel.

Evangelische Zentralstelle für Weltanschuungsfragen (The Evangelical Center for the Study of Worldview Questions). German Christian *countercult organization. Out of an acute awareness of the damage caused by *new religions in Germany in the years prior to 1945, this organization was founded in Stuttgart following World War II to act as a Christian *countercult organization. It relocated to Berlin in the mid-1990s and continues to produce various books, information leaflets and a magazine *(Materialdienst)* devoted to critiquing new religions from the perspective of Christian theology.

Evola, Julius (1898-1974). Fascist philosopher. Evola was a self-confessed Italian *fascist philosopher who wrote scathing attacks on democracy and American civilization that were couched in the terms of religious *mysticism. He was a member of the *traditionalist school of fascist philosophers founded by René *Guénon. His books in English translation include *Revolt Against the Modern World* (1996), *The Yoga of Power* (1993) and *The Mystery of the Grail* (1996).

evolution. The theory that life has evolved from lower to higher forms by means of a process of biological mutation and natural selection. In modern times the theory of evolution was first advanced by Charles Bonnet (1720-1793), who argued that an embryo already contains all the parts of the mature organism. Charles Lyell (1797-1874) speculated on the evolution of land animals in 1832, and his work influenced Charles *Darwin, who wrote *The Origin of Species* (1859). Prior to that, Herbert *Spencer in 1852 had defined a general theory of evolution from lower to higher forms of life and organization. What Darwin did was new: he described some of the processes by which new species developed and generalized these as natural selection. In the development of social Darwinism, the generalized theory of natural history provided images for social action and change and came to justify ruthless competition on the basis of "natural selection" and "the survival of the fittest." It was quickly adopted by *yogic thinkers, such Madame *Blavatsky and Swami *Vivekananda, who promoted a spiritualized form of evolution as an alternative to biblical accounts of human existence.

existential. An adjective frequently used in contemporary theological and religious literature to signify something that is of ultimate significance for one's being.

existentialism. A philosophical movement generally maintaining that human life is constituted by the choices one makes. Existentialism emerged as a movement in the late 1920s and was united by common concerns, motifs and emphases. The most influential exponents were the *Nazi thinker Martin *Heidegger, whose *Being and Time* appeared in 1927, the psychologist Karl *Jaspers, whose *Philosophie* appeared in 1932, and the French radical Jean Paul *Sartre. The movement began with the conviction that Western philosophy since the Greeks has been preoccupied with the idea of essence—that is, with the general and universal features of everything—rather than with concrete existence. Consequently, Western philosophy has been intellectualistic and rationalistic. It is, therefore, irrelevant as far as illuminating life is concerned because it obscures the truth about human existence.

exorcism. The act of casting out *demons or evil spirits in a *ritual designed to free the individual from evil influences. In the Orthodox Church exorcism is practiced prior to baptism. As a result of rationalism, in the nineteenth century belief in evil spirits was largely discarded by most Western churches. In recent years there has been a revival of the practice and an increasing demand for the services of exorcists by troubled individuals

F

FAIR. Family Action Information and Resource, a British *anticult movement. FAIR was founded in 1976 by concerned parents and others who were alarmed by the growth of *new religious movements. It rapidly became the main anticult movement in Britain and today publishes a regular newsletter that reviews the activities of new religions in Britain and elsewhere. FAIR also lobbies government departments and legislators to pass laws restricting the activities of new religions.

Falun Gong. A *new religion based on exercises intended as a form of *meditation. The name means "the practice of the wheel of dharma." (*See* dharma.) It was founded in 1992 by Li *Hongzhi, a Chinese immigrant to America living in New York. The group has incurred the wrath of the Chinese government because of its growing strength and the challenge it presents to the authorities.

Fard, Wallace D. (1877-c. 1934). Founder of the Nation of Islam. Fard was a Detroit clothes peddler who began teaching that he was a Muslim from Mecca with a message for black Americans. He went on to found the *Nation of Islam in 1930. He wrote several books, including *The Secret Ritual of the Nation of Islam in a Mathematical Way* (1933). He was regarded as a *prophet by his followers but vanished mysteriously in 1934. He was succeeded by Elijah *Muhammad as leader of the movement.

fascism. A powerful twentieth-century intellectual movement with religious roots and political aspirations. Fascism is often confused with *Nazism, and some use the word *fascism* as a mere propaganda device to discredit political opponents because of its association with *anti-Semitism. Actually, neither fascism nor Nazism is necessarily anti-Semitic, with the result that by renouncing anti-Semitism it is often possible for fascist thinkers to pass themselves off as conservatives or (less often) as radicals. Julius *Evola described fascism as a "revolt against the modern world," which, as Peter F. *Drucker pointed out, implied an attack on the middle class and the Jews in particular, who were seen as the ultimate representatives of middle-class and international values. Alfred *Rosenberg saw fascism as a movement of cultural and spiritual renewal that created a holistic sense of community. Contrary to popular Hollywood presentations, fascism was a highly intellectual movement that attracted many leading artists and thinkers. The movement found expression in the religious theories of René *Guénon, Jakob Wilhelm *Hauer, Martin *Heidegger, Ludwig *Klages, Alfred *Rosenberg and even Carl *Jung. Peter Drucker's *The End of Economic Man* (1939) is one of the best general accounts of fascism, while Zeev Sternhell's *The Birth of Fascist Ideology* (1994) examines its political theory. Various works by George L. Mosse, such as *The Nationalization of the Masses* (1975), and by Walter Laqueur, such as *Young Germany* (1962), examine the religious roots of fascism. Laqueur's *Fascism: Past, Present and Future* (1996) reminds us that it was an illusion to think that fascist influence ended with the Axis defeat in World War II. Still more chilling is Richard J. Golsan's *Fascism's Return: Scandal, Revision and Ideology Since 1980* (1998).

fate. The belief that human affairs are destined by cosmic powers, either God or gods or the workings of the universe.

Ferguson, Marilyn Grasso (1938-). Popular American publicist and advocate of *occult and *yogic religion. Ferguson first encountered these ideas through *Transcendental Meditation. Her best-selling book, *The Aquarian Conspiracy* (1980), was largely responsible for giving form to the *New Age movement and creating a consensus about its reality and importance as a spiritual force.

Feuerbach, Ludwig Andreas (1804-1872). German materialist philosopher. Feuerbach was influenced by Thomas *Paine, who is famous for his statement "A man is what he eats," which he used to explain English victories over Irish rebels. Feuerbach studied under G. W. F. Hegel (1770-1831), whose idealism he rejected in favor of a thoroughgoing materialism. Subsequently he attacked religious beliefs, especially those of Protestant Christianity as represented by Friedrich *Schleiermacher, by arguing that the idea of God is an outward projection of people's inner nature. Thus the Holy Family reflects the inadequacies of actual human families and subconsciously compensates for them in the imagination of the believer. His work had a profound influence on Karl Marx (1818-1883), who accepted and improved on Feuerbach's basic criticisms of religion with the result that he is usually described as a "left-wing Hegelian," whose thought is associated with thinkers on the radical left. Actually, Feuerbach's influence was arguably greater on the extreme right, where thinkers like Mathilda *Ludendorff (1877-1966), who founded a new "scientific" religion, accepted his views about immortality and the continuation of our existence through our race. Feuerbach also had a profound influence on the philosopher Friedrich *Nietzsche (1844-1900), whose work was also avidly read by right-wing radicals and National Socialists (*Nazis). His most-read books are *The Essence of Christianity* (1840) and *The Essence of Religion* (1846).

Findhorn Community. One of the most influential *New Age communities and a major source for the popularization of *neopaganism. The Findhorn Community was founded in 1965 by Eileen and Peter *Caddy in a desolate trailer park in northern Scotland. Since then it has acquired its own attractive grounds and a large country house. The success of the community is ascribed to *nature spirits. In 1970 an American, David *Spangler, joined the community and eventually became its main spokesperson and chief theorist. The philosophy of Findhorn is a mixture of *occult ideas of *theosophical origin.

folk religion. Popular religions, beliefs and practices, sometimes referred to as "little traditions,"which operate alongside of, and often in opposition to, a society's dominant religious tradition. Folk religions often involve *magic, healing, *prophetic movements and local *charismatic leaders or healers and are often regarded as a threat by the dominant tradition, which may take steps to suppress the practice of folk religion.

Fortune, Dion (1890-1946). Born Violet Firth, Fortune became the leading female figure in British *neopaganism during the first half of the twentieth century. She was a member of the *Order of the Golden Dawn and wrote numerous books, including *Esoteric Orders and Their Work* (1928).

Four Holy Truths. The four principles of existence discovered by the

Buddha. The Four Holy Truths are (1) suffering, (2) the cause of suffering, (3) the cessation of suffering and (4) the path that leads to the cessation of suffering. *See also* Dukkha (Pali)/Duhkha (Sanskrit).

Frazer, Sir James George (1854-1941). Social anthropologist. Frazer was a British lawyer who was influenced by William Robertson Smith and in 1907 became the first professor of social anthropology at the University of Liverpool, England. Frazer retired from this post to become a prolific writer. His "anthropology" was decidedly of the armchair variety, based on interpretations of works by missionaries, traders and travelers that tended to take beliefs and practices totally out of their social and historical context to create a grand theory. His influence on the development of comparative religion and popular religious ideas was considerable, as can be seen by the continuing popularity of his major work, *The Golden Bough* (published in twelve volumes between 1890 and 1915). This book was intended as an attack on Christianity, although actually it encouraged the growth of new religions. Today his work remains popular with the public but has little scholarly value.

Freemasonry. An international fraternal organization whose principles are embodied in symbols and allegories connected with the art of building and involving an oath of secrecy. The origins of the movement probably lie in twelfth-century Europe. There are two major divisions: the Old Charges, which date to 1390-1400; and the Masonic Word, which is a Scottish institution of obscure origin. From the eighteenth century, there developed "Speculative Masonry," or modern Freemasonry. The Grand Lodge was formed in 1717 to coordinate other lodges. The origins of most Masonic ceremonies are obscure and probably date to the seventeenth century. The movement places considerable emphasis on social welfare activities and claims to be based on the fundamentals of all religions. In the eighteenth century it was closely associated with *deism, and even today a deistic ethos generally prevails, modified by the incorporation of religious symbols derived from Assyrian and Egyptian beliefs. The Church of England, the Roman Catholic Church and many evangelical denominations have condemned Freemasonry as un-Christian. Recently various sensational journalists have published exposés, claiming that it is a closed club that often breaks the law to promote the interests of its members. Such claims are, of course, strongly denied by Masons.

Freud, Sigmund (1856-1939). Austrian neurologist and founder of psychoanalysis. Freud worked on the treatment of hysteria by hypnosis but later developed a method of treatment in which he replaced hyp-

nosis with free association of ideas. He believed that a complex of repressed and forgotten impressions underlies all abnormal mental
states, such as hysteria, and developed the theory that dreams are an
unconscious representation of repressed desires, especially of sexual
desires. Strongly anti-Christian, he authored *The Future of an Illusion*
(1927) and *Moses and Monotheism* (1939)—works that develop projec-
tionist theories similar to those of Ludwig *Feuerbach. In many respects his technique of psychoanalysis, which strongly influences
many new religions, can be seen as a form of secular *mysticism reminiscent of Jewish mystical thought.

Froebe (or Froebe-Kapteyn), Olga (1881-1979). English *Theosophist.
Froebe settled in Ascona, Switzerland, and with Alice *Bailey founded
the School of Spiritual Research in 1930. They separated shortly after-
ward because Bailey feared an "ancient evil" in the Ascona area,
where the school held its seminars. Subsequently Froebe approached
Rudolf *Otto and founded the *Eranos Seminar, which was launched
in 1933 with a lecture by Heinrich Zimmer (1890-1943) but was soon
dominated by Carl *Jung (1875-1961). After befriending Mary Mellon,
Froebe played a key role in the creation of the *Bollingen Foundation
and Series.

fundamentalism. Originally a movement of conservative Protestants
organized to resist theological liberalism. In the early twentieth century a conservative Christian movement arose in American Protestantism in opposition to *modernism. One of the movement's notable
achievements was the 1910 publication of *The Fundamentals*, a series of
tracts written by conservative scholars to counter certain theological
tendencies they considered dangerous. In a relatively short time the
fundamentalist image became stereotyped as close-minded, belliger-
ent, separatist and uncultured, even though some of the original fun-
damentalists were well-educated scholars. The term *fundamentalist* is
used today to describe a wide variety of conservative Protestant
groups, not all of whom are the direct heirs of the early movement. Recently the term *fundamentalism* has been applied to Hindus, Muslims
and members of other faiths who wish to retain their traditional beliefs
in the face of *modernity. Although there may be some merit in such
usage, it can be misleading because many people or groups identified
thus are simply anti-Western. For example, the Iranian revolution is
usually described as being "fundamentalist Islam," while the Saudis
are seen as pro-Western and therefore more liberal. In reality the Iranians interpret the Qur'an in a far more liberal and open manner than

the Saudis, who are much more analogous to Christian fundamental-
ists in their religious beliefs and practices than the Iranians. The use of
fundamentalism in this context is, therefore, not very helpful.

fundamentalist. A term originally applied to conservative Christians
who affirmed the fundamentals of the Christian faith. Today it is applied to almost anyone who holds conservative religious or moral
views.

G

Gaia. Name of the Greek earth goddess (Gea or Gaea), given by the
*New Age movement to the belief that the earth is a living organism.
Although on one level this notion is justified in terms of ecology, it is
in fact the revival of a medieval *occult idea that has been popularized
by *neopaganism and groups like the *Findhorn Community. Apart
from ideas about nature being alive, belief in such things as fairies and
*nature spirits is also connected with the idea.

Gandow, Thomas (1946-). Leader of the German *anticult movement
and the official expert on *cults and *sects for the *established Protestant church in Berlin-Brandenburg. He is the editor of *Berliner Dialog*
and author of several books, including one on cults and another on the
*Unification Church. Gandow is one of the people who persuaded the
German government to establish the *Enquete-Kommission in 1998
and has worked hard to support anticult legislation in other European
countries, including Russia. A deeply sincere man, he appears to be
motivated by the fact that new religions helped bring National Socialism (*Nazism) to power in the 1930s. Although his critiques are pene-
trating, they are marred by his contempt for scholars who show any
sympathy for new religions, such as Eileen *Barker and Gordon *Melton, and his lack of training in the history of religions. Consequently
he tends to see all new religions as dangerous while he supports any
traditional group. Thus he strongly attacks charismatic Christian
churches while appearing to approve of any actions of German Muslim groups. His attitudes also show the influence of a radical theological education that has no patience with traditional *orthodoxy, which
he labels *"fundamentalism."

Gardner, Gerald Brousseau (1884-1964). English Mason, *occultist and
creator of modern *witchcraft, or *Wicca. Gardner was a sickly child
and received little formal education. In 1900 he moved from England
to Sri Lanka, where he worked on a plantation and later became a civil

servant. He traveled widely in the East, absorbing local cultures and folk beliefs. Retiring to England in 1938, he joined a *theosophical group led by the daughter of Annie *Besant, through whom he claimed to have met Dorothy Clutterbuck, who he said was the witch who initiated him into "the craft." Recent research has cast doubt on this claim. In 1949, under the assumed name Scire, he published a novel called *High Magic's Aid*, where he outlined many of his ideas about magical ritual. (*See* magic; ritual.) Following the repeal of England's witchcraft laws in 1951, he published *Witchcraft Today* (1954) and numerous other books. Gardner's system is a mishmash of Masonic ritual, Eastern folk culture, *yogic religion and his own vivid imagination—all designed to appeal to a popular audience on the basis of its alleged historical roots. Central to his ideas is the creation of a *cult of the Mother Goddess, about whom he wrote in his novel *A Goddess Arrives* (1948). In 1963 Gardner initiated Raymond and Rosemary Buckland, who spread his creed to North America. *See also* Gardnerian witchcraft.

Gardnerian witchcraft. A *new religious movement that has influenced *Wicca and many *neopagan groups. It was created almost single-handedly by Gerald *Gardner (1884-1964), who attempted to recreate the type of *witchcraft discussed by Margaret *Murray in her various books. Gardner created rituals and beliefs by integrating older *occult and spiritualist ideas into a Gothic-type *mythology that drew on *yogic religions and his own rich imagination as well as Masonic rituals. Most important of all, Gardner supplied the *neopagan movement with pseudohistorical justifications, leading many to falsely believe that they were joining an ancient religion that had flourished underground despite being officially suppressed by Christianity. *See also* witchcraft.

Geller, Uri (1946-). Mind power advocate. Geller, an Israeli-born Austro-Hungarian and distant relative of Sigmund *Freud, has claimed mysterious powers whereby he is able to bend spoons and perform other unusual feats using the powers of his mind. He gained fame through numerous stage and television performances that led to successful tours of Europe and America. His demonstrations of mind power gave a great boost to the emerging *New Age and *esoteric movements. He was denounced by James Randi and other stage magicians who claimed that Geller is a trained *magician who has misused his skills to deceive rather than entertain.

Ghazali, al- (1059-1111). Islamic theologian and *mystic. Ghazali, who became the most original thinker and greatest theologian of Islam, as a youth tended toward rationalism before becoming a complete *skeptic. He recovered his faith through *Sufism and mystical experiences.

Gibran, Kahlil (1883-1931). Lebanese *mystic, poet and playwright. Gibran abandoned Arabic for English as his preferred language in order to express his mystical visions in a series of books. Many of these books, such as *Jesus the Son of Man* (1928), have Christian-sounding themes. His best-known work is *The Prophet* (1923). Often proclaimed a *Sufi master by his followers, he was in fact an unhappy man who preached an *eclectic creed lacking real substance. He died of alcoholism.

Glastonbury. New Age center. Glastonbury is a small town in England, the site of a large ruined monastery where King Arthur is said to be buried. Before the Reformation, its Benedictine monastery was the largest in England and traced its ancestry to an ancient church building that the monks claimed was built by Joseph of Arimathea following the execution and resurrection of Jesus. Many medieval *legends, including ones about visits by the child Jesus, are associated with the town. In the 1960s it became a center for the *counterculture movement and has since played a prominent role in the mythology of the *New Age movement and modern *esoteric spirituality.

global culture. A transnational or transsocietal network of cosmopolitan people who self-consciously cultivate an openness to diverse cultures. Global cultures are meaning networks, or transnational webs of meaning, that express global dimensions. Global cultures transcend national, international, ethnic, racial and class boundaries to create a new whole. They are, paradoxically, local cultures because they always grow out of and incorporate local beliefs and practices, whose participants inhabit the globe. Many *new religions blend elements from global and local cultures to create their own unique system of beliefs and practices.

Gnosticism. A popular religious and philosophical movement of the Greco-Roman world. Gnostic groups were characterized by their claim to possess secret knowledge—*gnosis*—about the nature of the universe and human existence. Despite what seem to be clear criticisms of Gnostic-type ideas in the New Testament, many writers have attempted to prove a link between the early Christian church and Gnosticism. This view has been increasingly discredited as our knowledge of both Gnosticism and the early church has increased through archaeological and other discoveries, such as the *Nag Hammadi scrolls. Today it seems almost certain that Gnosticism did not arise until the second century A.D. and found expression in many different sects and settings. Many *New Age-type groups claim links to ancient Gnosticism, although such claims are pure fabrication.

Gobind Singh (1666-1708). The tenth Sikh guru, who gave the community its present form. Gobind Singh organized the Sikhs as an effective military force and ordained the "Five Emblems," or "Five Ks," of *Sikhism. Before he was assassinated in 1708, he made his followers accept that he was the last human guru and that after his death they would look to their sacred writings, the *Granth,* as their guru.

Gobineau, Comte Joseph Arthur de (1816-1882). French diplomat and father of modern racism. Gobineau's theories, which included Nordic supremacy and *anti-Semitism, involved a rejection of orthodox Christianity and have had a disastrous effect on European history. *See also* biological racism.

Goethe, Johann Wolfgang von (1749-1832). German poet and philosopher. In his early work Goethe was an exponent of *Romanticism, but later he took a more critical attitude toward the Romantic movement and developed his own unique insights and spirituality. A lover of nature, he was a religious humanist who strongly influenced German culture. Many creators of *new religions have been indirectly influenced by Goethe's thought, which blends scientific interests with spirituality to create a form of *pantheism.

Graves, Robert (1895-1985). English author. Graves is best known for his *I, Claudius* books and television series. But his book *The White Goddess* (1948) played an important role in the revival of *neopaganism, which he actively promoted. He was a friend of Gerald *Gardner.

Great Mother. Ancient goddess. The Great Mother was the central figure in a Greek cult that became important in the Roman Empire before dying out around the fourth century. Many *Wicca-type movements have sought to revive the Great Mother cult by giving it modern interpretations in terms of a feminist theology.

Great White Brotherhood. An imaginary hierarchy of spiritual beings, who were said to oversee human development. The idea is important in *Theosophy and many of its offshoots, such as the *I-Am movement. According to Helena *Blavatsky, the brotherhood is based in Tibet, from where it contacts initiates by telepathy.

Groothuis, Douglas R. (1957-). Philosopher and New Age critic. Groothuis teaches philosophy at Denver Seminary and is author of *Unmasking the New Age* (1986), which was one of the first evangelical books to deal seriously with the *New Age movement

Guénon, René (1886-1951). Founder and chief theorist of the *tradition-alist school of fascist philosophers. Guénon's main work combines re-ligious speculation with political theorizing and explicit racism. In 1930 he moved to Cairo, where he remained until his death, taking an Arab name and claiming to be a Sufi master. The traditionalist school included Julius *Evola, Frithjof *Schuon, Mircea *Eliade, Ananda *Coomaraswamy and, as a fringe member, Joseph *Campbell. Guénon's books include *The Crisis of the Modern World* (1927) and *Intro-duction to the Study of Hindu Doctrine* (1921).

Gurdjieff, George Ivanovitch (1872-1949). Russian spiritual teacher. Gurdjieff was of Greek descent, and his biography is reminiscent of Helena *Blavatsky's. He fled Russia in 1917 and settled in Paris before establishing his Institute for the Harmonious Development of Man near Fontainebleau in 1922. There he developed a form of dancing meditation. His institute closed in 1933, and he began life as a traveling teacher who frequently visited America, where he promoted a highly secretive system of *occult knowledge.

H

Hadden, Jeffrey K. (1924-). American sociologist of religion who coined the term *televangelism*. Hadden, a professor of sociology at the Univer-sity of Virginia, is the author of numerous books, including *Televange-lism, Power and Politics* (1988). In recent years he has devoted himself to developing an extensive website that provides basic information on *new religions and detailed academic discussions of particular topics.

Haekel, Ernst (1834-1919). German scientist and disciple of Charles *Darwin. Haekel's numerous books promote Darwin's theory of *evo-lution. He founded the *Monist League as a modern *scientific religion and developed the theory of *Lemuria, an ancient or lost continent from which humans evolved. Helena *Blavatsky blended Haekel's ideas about *Lemuria with Ignatius *Donnelly's writings about *At-lantis to create her own theory of human spiritual development.

Hare Krishna movement. The International Society for Krishna Con-sciousness (ISKCON), founded on his arrival in America in 1965 by His Divine Grace Swami A. C. Bhaktivedanta *Prabhupada, and one of the most visible of the *new religious movements. Devotees, wear-ing saffron-colored robes, sing and dance and sell recordings, books and the magazine *Back to Godhead*. The young men have their heads shaved, apart from a topknot, by which they believe *Krishna will pluck them up when he rescues them at the time of the deliverance of the world. It is through the frequent chanting of their *mantra—"Hare Krishna, Hare Krishna"—that the devotees have become popularly known as Hare Krishnas. The theological basis of the movement is the Bhagavad-Gita as translated by their master. They publish numerous books, many of which are translations of Hindu religious classics, and the academic journal *Iskon Communications Journal,* which often carries valuable articles written by scholars who are not members of the movement.

harmonic convergence. An alignment of stars and planets said to release cosmic energies. The idea of a harmonic convergence is believed to have originated with Jose Arguelles in his book *The Transformative Vision* (1975). He claimed the idea is based on prophecies from ancient *Mayan writings that predicted the release of cosmic energies due to a cyclic alignment of various stars and planets. Arguelles argued that this would occur on August 16 and 17, 1987. Many people in the *New Age movement latched on to this idea, which since then has been closely linked with the *Gaia hypothesis and an expectation of imminent spiritual and social change.

Harris, William Wade, the Prophet (1865-1929). Liberian evangelist and church founder. Harris was an Anglican lay preacher who traveled to the Ivory Coast in 1913 wearing a white gown with black bands crossed on the chest. He carried a gourd for baptismal water, a rattle and a large staff in the form of a cross. His dynamic preaching and call for people to forsake their traditional beliefs and accept Christ led to a major revival and the foundation of many *Harrist churches. He was deported from the Ivory Coast by the French authorities at the end of 1914 after having baptized over 120,000 people, whom he had begun to organize into a church with the help of Methodists. After his expulsion, he returned to Liberia, from where he continued to guide (though not directly) his followers.

Harrison, Paul (1945-). The English founder of *scientific pantheism.

Harrist churches. Independent church movement founded by the Prophet *Harris. In 1913 and 1914 a revival broke out in the Ivory Coast—a predominantly Roman Catholic and Muslim country—in response to the preaching of the Prophet Harris. As a result, the French colonial authorities deported the prophet to his native Liberia at the end of 1914, and his followers were left leaderless, with only a rudimentary organization based on Methodism. Harris had, however, made a prophecy about the arrival of Bible teachers. In 1924 the long-awaited teachers arrived in the form of Protestant missionaries, who were welcomed by Harris's followers. Tensions soon developed over African cultural traditions, especially polygamy, and with the blessing of the Prophet, his followers formed their own churches. Today the Harrist churches form a large family of West African Christians in a number of different church groups. Their theology is orthodox in intent, although it is deeply colored by their experience of colonialism and African culture. *See also* African independent churches.

Hasidic Jews. Followers of *Hasidism or Hasidic practices.

Hasidism. Hebrew term for "piety" or "the pious." In the eighteenth century Hasidism became associated with an Eastern European Jewish *sect founded by Rabbi Israel ben Eliezer. It reacted against what it saw as the arid interpretation of the Talmud by rabbis and drew on the *cabala to develop a rich mystical tradition. *Hasdic Jews seek union with God through ecstatic prayer, and they earnestly desire the coming of the Messiah. Today Martin *Buber is the best-known interpreter of Hasidism, even though many scholars question his understanding of the tradition.

hatha yoga. The branch of *yoga that seeks to establish conscious control over the automatic processes of the body. Hatha yoga is the most popular form of yoga in the West, where it is taught in terms of physical health and exercise. Hatha yoga is often mistakenly thought by Westerners to be the only form of yoga.

Hauer, Jakob Wilhelm (1881-1962). National Socialist and leader of the German Faith movement. A former Christian missionary, Hauer lost his faith and later became professor of religious studies at the University of Tübingen and leader of the *Deutscher Glaubensbewegung,* or German Faith movement, which he saw as the religious foundation for National Socialism (*Nazism) and an alternative to the spiritual ideas of Alfred *Rosenberg. Hauer influenced many students and other young people to join the National Socialist Party through his skillful cultivation of an apparent academic neutrality that he maintained by denying that he was a National Socialist and concealing his membership in the SS from the uninitiated. Hauer corresponded with Mircea *Eliade (although most of those letters have conveniently disappeared) and apparently met with him after the war. He also collaborated with Carl *Jung, with whom he sometimes cotaught seminars on religion and psychology. Hauer's religious views were strongly influenced by *yogic religions and his keen interest in *myth. Horst Junginger has published a scholarly study on Hauer in German, while Karla

Poewe and Werner Ustorf are working on studies in English.

Heaven's Gate. UFO cult. Heaven's Gate was a small and rather insig-
nificant UFO cult founded in 1975 by Marshall *Applewhite and Bonnie Lu *Nettles after several extensive tours of the West Coast of
America during which they proclaimed themselves messengers of a
UFO mission to earth. The group achieved notoriety in 1997 when, after advertising their plans on the Internet, they all committed suicide
in a *ritual act intended to take their souls to a UFO that they believed
was hiding in the tail of the Hale-Bopp comet.

Heidegger, Martin (1889-1976). German existentialist philosopher.
Heidegger was a central figure in contemporary Continental philosophy whose work shaped the development of *existentialism, herme-
neutics and, more recently, postmodernism and deconstruction. In his
key work, *Being and Time* (1927), on which his reputation rested, he
characterized everyday existence as inauthentic because we are
thrown into our world, or mental universe, which makes our self in-
separable from our world and, as a result, genuine being remains un-
discovered. Although his philosophy appeared deeply spiritual, he
strongly attacked Christianity for contributing to our self-betrayal and
what he saw as the destruction of genuine culture. As early as 1946,
Karl Lowith pointed out Heidegger's enthusiasm for the *Nazis. This
accusation was vigorously denied by his followers but now seems established beyond all doubt since the publication of Hugo Ott's *Martin
Heidegger: A Political Life* (1994). Ott's work proves that Heidegger was
and remained a Nazi until at least the end of World War II. Even more
devastating is the argument of Johannes Fritsche, who in *Historical
Destiny and National Socialism in Heidegger's Being and Time* (1999) dem-
onstrates that *Being and Time* shares a common intellectual structure
with Hitler's *Mein Kampf* and that the entire argument is rooted in National Socialist ideology. Finally, any remaining admiration for
Heidegger as a scholar has been destroyed by the publication of Rein-
hard May's little-known *Heidegger's Hidden Sources* (1996), which
shows that the philosopher "appropriated" without acknowledgment
key sections for his major work, *Being and Time,* from forgotten German translations of Chinese and Japanese texts, some of which were
actually translated by Martin *Buber. Put straightforwardly, Heidegger was a plagiarist.

heresy. In its loose sense this term refers to the conscious, willful rejection of any doctrine held to be normative by a group or institution. Roman Catholicism defines a heretic as any baptized person who,

wishing to call himself or herself a Christian, denies the truth revealed to the church. Until the nineteenth century, Protestants generally regarded heresy as the willful rejection of any truth taught in the Bible. With the rise of *biblical criticism, defining heresy became a problem because the notion of a canon and of *orthodoxy itself was undermined. Although originally a religious term, it is common today to talk about political, scientific and other forms of "heresy" to mean deviation from the status quo or accepted ideas.

Hesse, Hermann (1877-1962). German poet and novelist. Born of a missionary family in India, Hesse rejected Christianity and was deeply influenced by Søren Kierkegaard (1813-1855), Friedrich *Nietzsche (1844-1900) and Buddhism. His works became cult readings among American West Coast hippies during the 1960s. The hallmark of his work is a desire for experience, untrammeled by the inhibitions of institutionalized society, to elicit a liberation of thought and behavior. His most famous works are *Siddhartha* (1922; English translation, 1951), *Steppenwolf* (1927; English translation, 1929) and *The Glass Bead Game* (1943; English translation, 1970).

holiness. The essential character of God in Christian theology and a key concept in many new spiritual traditions, where it is often understood as a form of power.

holism. A term used by General Jan *Smuts in his book *Holism and Evolution* (1926) to express his belief in *emergent evolution. The idea comes from idealist philosophy and expresses the notion of wholeness. In recent years it has become a buzzword in various *alternative health movements and the *New Age movement.

homeopathy. An *alternative medicine. Homeopathy is a nineteenth-century alternative to allopathy, or medicine that uses drugs. It is based on the principle that like cures like. Homeopaths use very small doses of specially prepared essences to treat illness. In North America homeopathy is generally considered quackery. In Britain it is part of the National Health scheme due to the support of the royal family. In Germany it is generally accepted alongside allopathic medicine and is promoted by groups such as *anthroposophy.

Hubbard, L. Ron (1911-1976). Founder of *Scientology. Hubbard was a brilliant science fiction writer and adventurer who in 1955 proceeded to found his own *scientific religion, Scientology. His bestselling *Dianetics: The Modern Science of Mental Health* (1951) provided the basis for this *new religion, while his science fiction novels were to provide it with a rich *mythology and understanding of human history. (*See* dianetics.) Hubbard was an American individualist who appears to have been influenced by Herbert *Spencer.

Hunke, Sigrid (1913-2000). German author and neopagan leader. Hunke was the founder of various *neopagan religious groups associated with the *Freie Religiouse,* or the Free Religious movement, and onetime president of the *Deutscher Unitarier* (German Unitarians). Her book *Allahs Sonne über dem Abendland* (*Allah's Son over the West,* 1960) won her Egypt's highest literary award and an honorary seat on the Supreme Council for Islamic Affairs in Cairo in 1974. Her books *Europas ander Religion* (*Europe's Other Religion,* 1969) and *Europas Eigene Religion* (*Europe's Own Religion,* 1997) popularized the notion that Christianity is an alien tradition to Europe and attempted to trace the "true" European religion through a long line of people she identified, sometimes quite wrongly, as heretics. A former Nazi Youth leader, Hunke's religious theories are almost identical with theories propagated by *Nazi apologists, including Alfred *Rosenberg and Jakob *Hauer. The big difference between her views and those of Nazi writers is that she replaced references to Germany and the German tradition with Europe, and references to the Jews with statements about Christianity as a form of cultural imperialism imposed on Europeans by early Christian missionaries. Although her work is little known in English, she was a best-selling author in Germany, and her work is the subject of an ongoing study by Karla Poewe.

Huxley, Aldous Leonard (1894-1963). English mystical writer novelist, essayist and poet. Aldous Huxley was the grandson of T. H. *Huxley and is best known for his book *Brave New World* (1932). He experimented with drug-induced states to achieve spiritual insight, and his writings were popular in the 1960s *counterculture. *See also* mysticism.

Huxley, Thomas Henry (1825-1895). English biologist and *agnostic who was an advocate of scientific training to remedy the intellectual, social and moral needs of humanity.

I

I-Am Movement. A movement of Theosophical origin founded by Guy *Ballard, dating to his revelatory experiences with "ascended masters" in 1930. The movement became public in 1937 and gave birth to various groups, including the Church Universal and Triumphant.

iconic leader. Someone who is perceived as a concrete representation or *revelation of the *holy.

INFORM. Information Network Focus on Religious Movements. Founded in 1988 by Eileen *Barker to promote understanding between members of new religions and interested outside parties, such as family members and the media. It has been recognized by the British government as providing a valuable public service, but Barker and the movement have been opposed by anticult activists, who have spread false claims about INFORM through the internet and other channels.

Irving, Edward (1792-1834). Founding figure of the Catholic Apostolic Church. Irving was a Scottish Presbyterian who in 1822 became minister of Caledonian Chapel in London, where he became known for his opposition to political reform, Catholic emancipation and the University of London, which he called "the synagogue of Satan." Irving also embraced millennial ideas and encouraged speaking in tongues and charismatic gifts. (*See* millennialism.) A church schism ensued in 1832, and Irving's followers formed the *Catholic Apostolic Church. His writings include *The Coming of the Messiah in Glory and Majesty* (1827), *For the Oracles of God* (1832) and *The Orthodox and Catholic Doctrine of Our Lord's Human Nature* (1830).

Isis. Ancient Egyptian goddess. Isis was the wife of Osiris and mother of Horus and was often depicted as a woman suckling a child. Her *cult was popular throughout the Greco-Roman world and bears resemblance to the cult of the Virgin Mary. *See also* Egyptian religions.

Islam. The faith, obedience and practice of the followers of *Muhammad, believed by them to be the final and perfected religion revealed by God. Today there are over one billion Muslims in the world. They recognize biblical figures such as Abraham, Moses and Jesus as prophets whose followers have distorted their revelations, an idea that is believed to be taught by the Qur'an but in actuality dates from Muslim teaching in its fourth century. Orthodox Islam is rooted in the observance of five rituals: weekly communal worship, daily devotions, a monthlong fast (Ramadan), payment of a religious tax and at least one pilgrimage to Mecca, an Islamic holy city. To these duties is added Jihad, "religious striving." Some interpret this as a warlike defense of Islam, while others count Jihad as an internal, personal struggle against sin. Islam makes no distinction between the secular and the sacred. Though several formerly Muslim countries such as Turkey have experimented with secular government, such experiments have been rejected by orthodox Muslims. *See also* Nation of Islam.

Ismalis. A dynamic and essentially liberal, sectarian *Islamic movement which teaches that the Qur'an has an internal as well as an external meaning. There are various grades of members and associates, with the higher grades receiving more *esoteric teaching than that of traditional Islam. The leader of the movement, the Aga Khan, claims descent from *Muhammad. The movement has proved to be highly adaptable in bringing its ancient beliefs into the context of modern society.

isvar. A *Sanskrit word meaning "lord" that is used to refer to God as the supreme personal being and is frequently used in *bhakti. Usually the Lord is identified with Vishnu, Siva or *Brahman, or even all three together. The Lord is thought of as the creator of the world and often as its destroyer.

I-thou. A posture of openness, receptivity and engagement. The Jewish philosopher Martin *Buber, in his poem-book *I and Thou* (1937), distinguished between two basic attitudes—those that people assume toward beings and those that they assume toward things. The two postures are represented symbolically by two primary terms, "I-thou" and "I-it." "I-thou" implies openness and a personal relationship, while "I-it" suggests a cold objectivity and detachment. These terms entered the vocabulary of many spiritual gurus in the 1960s.

J

Jainism. Indian ascetic religion. Jainism probably dates to at least the eighth century B.C., although most Western scholars trace its founding to Mahvira in the sixth century B.C. A highly conservative movement, it stresses asceticism and holds beliefs similar to those of Buddhism and the Hindu tradition, its main rivals. The universe is conceived of as an everlasting succession of heavens and hells to which all beings are bound by *karma and from which liberation is desirable through ascetic practice. The *Osho movement of *Bhagwan Sri Rajneesh is a new religion that originated within the Jain tradition.

Jamaa. Roman Catholic revitalization movement in Africa. The Swahili word for "family" was adopted by Father Placide Tempels (1906-1977), a Franciscan missionary, for the highly successful *revitalization movement he founded within the Roman Catholic Church in Zaire in the late 1930s and 1940s. Tempels outlined his basic outlook in *Bantu Philosophy* (1959), where he emphasized human dignity, a sense of community and the need to take African tradition seriously. (*See* African traditional religions.) The movement spread rapidly, took on a life of its own and gave rise to tensions between the membership and the church hierarchy. Ill health caused Tempels to leave the Congo in

1962. Today various forms of the Jamaa movement continue within and without the Roman Catholic Church.

James, William (1842-1910). Philosopher and psychologist of religion. William James was the brother of the American novelist Henry James (1843-1916), and their father was a *Swedenborgian theologian. James was successively professor of psychology (1889-1897) and professor of philosophy (1897-1907) at Harvard University. His book *The Varieties of Religious Experience* (1902) laid the basis for the psychology of religion, while his *Pragmatism* (1907) strongly influenced the development of American thought during the first half of the twentieth century.

Jaspers, Karl (1883-1969). German *existentialist philosopher. Jaspers practiced psychiatry and then moved via psychology to philosophy, finally accepting a professorship at Heidelberg in 1921. He was ousted from his post during the Nazi era but returned after the war. In *Nietzsche and Christianity* (1946), *The Perennial Scope of Theology* (1948) and *Myth and Christianity* (1954) Jaspers saw religious answers emerging from metaphysical descriptions of being. He rejected theism, *pantheism, revealed religion and *atheism as mere ciphers or symbols that should not be taken literally, and he argued that one should look to phenomenological descriptions of the fringes of inner and outer experiences for understanding. Less influential than the teachings of Carl *Jung, his work has nevertheless influenced many *new religions with a psychological basis, such as *Osho.

Jehovah's Witnesses. A highly rationalist, *adventist and pacifist *sect founded by Charles Taze Russell (1852-1916) in the late nineteenth century. It originally mixed a blend of interpretation of biblical *prophecy with *pyramidology and various other *esoteric teachings to foretell the end of the world. As the theology developed, Jehovah's Witnesses progressively rejected orthodox Christian beliefs, such as the Trinity and incarnation of Christ, and developed a unique deistic theology similar to ancient *Arianism. They totally reject the theory of *evolution as well as blood transfusions.

Joachim of Fiore (c. 1135-1202). Medieval *mystic and writer of *apocalyptic works. Joachim experienced a religious conversion on a pilgrimage to Jerusalem and later entered the Cistercian Order. After a short spell as abbot of Corazzo, he resigned to devote himself to apocalyptic writings, which develop an elaborate interpretation of history involving three stages based on the persons of the Trinity. He said little about the third phase, or age of the Spirit, except that it would see the rise of new religious orders that would convert the whole world. But it became the focus of speculation in the movement known as *Joachimism. The spiritual Franciscans, various Protestant groups and, in recent times, the *New Age movement have all been influenced by his work.

Joachimism. A medieval *apocalyptic movement based on the works of *Joachim of Fiore that developed a forward-looking *eschatology anticipating the Age of the Spirit.

Jodo. A Japanese school of *Pure Land Buddhism. Jodo was founded by Honen (1133-1212), who proclaimed Amida the Buddha of Infinite Light and Great Compassion. It became the most popular form of Buddhism in Japan. Under *Shinran (disciple of Honen), it developed into Jodo-Shinshu, which proclaimed the doctrine of tariki, or "other power," which offered salvation by grace and faith through the recitation of Amida's name. Through trust in the vow of Amida to save all sentient beings who called on him, devotees were promised *rebirth in the western paradise, from where they would achieve liberation.

Jojitsu. A minor school of Buddhism. Jojitsu was introduced to Japan by Korean monks around A.D. 625. It is nihilistic in tone, being based on a study of cosmology and psychology strongly influenced by Hindu thinkers such as Nagarjuna and Deva. It teaches that the ego and all dharmas are equally illusory. Furthermore, it conceives the past and future as nonexistent, while the present vanishes as soon as it occurs.

Jones, Jim (1931-1978). Founder of the People's Temple. Jones was a minister of the Disciples of Christ when he founded the *People's Temple, in Ukiah, California. In 1977 Jones moved with a number of his followers to Guyana, in South America, where they formed a colony known as Jonestown. The movement became notorious in November 1978 when Jones and his followers committed mass suicide. A professed Marxist, Jones was active in numerous left-wing causes and was widely respected for his social work before his bizarre suicide.

Journal for the Scientific Study of Religion. The official academic journal of the Society for the Scientific Study of Religion. It carries numerous articles on the sociology of religions, many of which deal with *new religious movements.

Journal of Contemporary Religion. A leading British academic journal that focuses on the study of new religions.

Jung, Carl Gustav (1875-1961). Swiss psychiatrist. Jung developed his own system of psychology, characterized by strong religious and *occult overtones drawn from *alchemy, *yogic religions and various *esoteric traditions. He developed a theory of *archetypes—a form of *pseudoscience rejected by modern psychiatry, although popular with many religious and literary writers. Jung also worked and shared many ideas with Jakob *Hauer, although they eventually disagreed over Jung's *occult interests. Jung's works include *Psychology and Alchemy* (1953). Richard Noll, in *The Jung Cult* (1994), discusses the religious dimensions of Jung's work.

K

kama. Indian term for "pleasure" or "sensual enjoyment." It is one of the four traditional ends, or aims, of life in Hindu thought and enters *New Age thinking through texts like the erotic *Kama Sutra.*

karma. Literally "action," it is an eternal law of cosmic cause and effect, or acts and deeds, which form the destiny of individuals. Karma is usually understood as the means by which a person's fate is determined by past actions. Karma is complex and has many levels of meaning but has been popularized in the West as a way of understanding *fate.

Kimbangist Church. One of the largest *African independent churches. The church grew out of a movement that originated in the preaching of Simon *Kimbangu. Following Kimbangu's imprisonment in 1921, hundreds of people claimed to receive visions in which he preached to them the gospel of Jesus Christ. This led to the founding of numerous new churches. Today it is one of the largest religious organizations in Africa and a member of the World Council of Churches.

Kimbangu, Simon (1887?-1951). African *prophet and independent church founder. Converted by the Baptist Missionary Society in 1915, Kimbangu later claimed to have received a *vision of Jesus in which he was commanded to preach and heal. After preaching and healing for a few months in 1921, he had established a large movement in the Belgian Congo that was perceived as a threat by Belgian authorities. He was arrested and spent the rest of his life in prison. However, people began to see him in dreams, and his movement spread. *See also* Kimbangist Church.

King Arthur. Legendary king of ancient Britain. Among other things, Arthur is said to have been spirited away by mystical maidens before his death. His body is believed to be buried in the *Glastonbury area, from where he will emerge to restore order when England faces its darkest hour. Legends about Arthur play an important role in many *occult movements, from the writings of Julius *Evola to the hippies in Glastonbury.

King, George (1919-1997). Founder of the Aetherius Society. King was an English taxi driver who became influenced by *theosophical teachings. In 1956 he founded the *Aetherius Society after claiming he was contacted telepathically by extraterrestrials. In latter years he styled himself "Sir George King" and claimed innumerable honors and university degrees.

Klages, Ludwig (1872-1956). German psychologist and graphologist. Klages was a *völkisch* irrationalist who was taught evolutionary vitalism and believed that handwriting reveals character. He coined many of the key terms of postmodernism—for example, *logozentrismus* (logocentrism)—and promoted *fascist views linked to *theosophical-type religious movements.

Knight, J. Z. (1946-). American *occultist and channeler. Knight claims to be the medium through whom an ancient spirit entity from *Atlantis named *Ramtha communicates with humanity. Raised in a fundamentalist Christian home, she dabbled in the *occult and drifted into *spiritualism before developing her own unique teachings. She is the founder of Ramtha's School of Enlightenment in Yelm, Washington. Shirley *Maclaine was one of her many clients.

koan. A *Zen Buddhist term referring to an exercise given by a Zen master to a disciple designed to break his or her intellectual limitations and produce a sudden flash of *enlightenment.

Koestler, Arthur (1905-1983). Hungarian Jewish novelist and journalist. Koestler developed strong interests in the paranormal, and his book *The Lotus and the Robot* (1966) is a telling critique of Indian spirituality and its Western counterparts.

Konko Kyo. *Shinto sect. Founded in 1859 by Kawate Bunjiro (1814-1883), the *sect seeks to revitalize Shintoism for contemporary society. The name means "Golden Lustered Teaching." It emphasizes one God and good health as a result of fellowship with God, and it repudiates superstition associated with *ritual practice and *magical charms.

Koresh, David (1959-1993). Leader of the *Branch Davidians. Koresh's life ended when he and his followers died in a fire that engulfed their Waco, Texas, community on April 19, 1993, after a long siege by federal agents.

Krebs, Pierre (1943-). French cultural critic. Krebs is editor of *Elemente* and a leading neofascist writer who articulates a coherent theory of cultural criticism that recognizes the importance of religion in cultural change. (*See* fascism.) His books include *Im Kampf um das Wesen* (*The War for Essence*, 1997).

Krishna. The most important incarnation of the god Vishnu in Hindu
*mythology. The name literally means "the Black One." The stories of
the *Mahabharata are about aspects of Krishna's earthly existence, the
most important spiritual section of which is the *Bhagavad-Gita. Legends about Krishna abound and often contain erotic love stories. Other
accounts involve his rescue from a massacre of children and death by
an arrow that struck his heel, his only vulnerable spot. Some scholars
see these latter stories as reflecting influence from the Christian Gos-
pels and Greek mythology about Achilles. Others suggest that the
Krishna stories are based on an actual historical figure who later came
to be considered a god.

Krishnamurti, Jiddu (1895-1986). Indian *mystic. From the age of
twelve, he was reared and educated by Charles W. Leadbeater (1847-
1934), Annie *Besant (1847-1933) and other *Theosophists at Adyar,
outside Madras, India, to prepare him to become the next world teacher. A fever of excitement built up in the 1920s as the *Theosophical Society geared itself up for the expected manifestation of Maitreya
through Krishnamurti. But the period of preparation culminated in a
series of shattering psychic and physical experiences for Krishnamurti
that led him to reject all religions, philosophies and preconceptions
about *enlightenment. In 1929 he parted company with the Theosophical Society and began teaching a kind of therapeutic dialectic.

kundalini. A feminine serpent power that plays an important role in
*tantra. According to traditional Hindu physiology, it is believed to
coil itself around the lingam, thus preventing the movement of vital
powers toward the head. When awakened by *yoga, tremendous heat
is produced and the *yogi can gain purification and power, which ultimately result in liberation. Kundalini is also identified with the
coiled serpent power that gave birth to the universe.

L

Lagarde, Paul Anton de (1827-1891). German Protestant biblical critic.
Lagarde was mentor to the famous biblical critic Julius Wellhausen
(1844-1918) and was called by Alfred *Rosenberg "the prophet" of the
German people. (*See* biblical criticism.) Lagarde was intensely *anti-
Semitic, and his writings developed the theme that Germans needed
to create or rediscover their own religion. These ideas encouraged
Friedrich *Nietzsche, Erich *Ludendorff and numerous others to look
beyond Christianity for a new religion.

Leary, Timothy (1920-1996). American psychologist and guru of the 1960s drug culture. (*See* counterculture.) Leary is famous for his saying "Turn on, tune in and drop out." He was the author of various books, such as *The Politics of Ecstasy* (1970), in which he advocated a drug-induced spirituality.

Lee, Ann (1736-1784). Shaker leader. Originally a Shaking Quaker in Manchester, England, Lee withdrew from her husband in 1766 and assumed leadership of the local Shakers. Her cardinal doctrines were confession as the door to the regenerate life and celibacy as its rule and cross. "Mother Ann, the Word" (as she was called) and seven followers emigrated from England to New York in 1774, and the movement then grew rapidly. She formulated the characteristic beliefs of the *Shakers: celibacy, communism, pacifism, *millennialism, elitism and spiritual manifestations through barking, dancing and shaking.

Lee, Witness (1905-1997). Chinese Christian spiritual leader. Witness Lee was a follower of Watchman Nee in China who moved to Taiwan in 1949 and then to southern California in 1962. He was founder of *Local Church—a controversial movement that encourages a form of communal living and various liturgical practices such as "prayer reading" of the Bible. Lee was accused of *heresy by many other Christians because of his teachings about the incarnation and the Trinity, but his followers vigorously denied the charge. Lee published numerous works and established Living Stream Ministry in Anaheim, California.

legend. Traditional stories from the distant past. Legends usually deal with cultural heroes and significant events in the life of a people. They are often woven into the fabric of new religions. *See also* myth.

Lemuria. A "lost" ancient culture. Lemuria was an invention borrowed by Helena *Blavatsky from the scientific work of Ernst *Haekel, who posited Lemuria as one of the sources of ancient civilizations such as that of the Egyptians. It was supposedly located in the South Pacific and was contemporaneous with *Atlantis. Others have called it *Mu.

Li, Hongzhi (1951/1952-). Founder of *Falun Gong. His date of birth is in dispute because he claims that the Chinese government altered his birth certificate when it was discovered that his birthday was also the birthday of the historical Buddha. A controversial figure, he now lives in America.

Local Church. A controversial *new religious movement founded by Witness *Lee, a follower of Watchman Nee. The group is strongly influenced by the theology of the Plymouth Brethren, especially the writings of J. Nelson Darby. Its ongoing ministry is carried out by Living Stream Ministry in Anaheim, California.

Lotus Sutra. Probably the most important text of Mahayana *Buddhism. Its rich mythology and doctrine inspired the development of *Pure Land Buddhism and a variety of other Buddhist *sects in China and Japan. It stresses the omniscience and eternal power of the Buddha.

Lubavitch Hasidism. A Jewish *revitalization movement. Lubavitch Hasidism originated in Lithuania in 1773 through the ministry of Rabbi *Zalman. In the 1920s it spread to North America, where it remains active in the Jewish community. The Lubavitch have *orthodox Jewish theological beliefs, to which they add a strong emphasis on the observance of Jewish laws and messianic expectations. *See also* Hasidism.

Ludendorff Bewegung. A German *new religious movement (*bewegung* means "movement"), also called *Gotterkenntnis* ("God-consciousness"). The Ludendorff Bewegung was founded by Mathilda von *Kemnitz in 1919, based on "scientific principles." (*See* Ludendorff, Mathilda.) Kemnitz was highly critical of both the *occult and Christianity, which she saw as an alien religion imposed on the German people by missionaries. Gender equality, an acceptance of *fate and the belief that immortality is found in one's descendants were important elements in her teachings. She scorned Jews, *Freemasons and liberals alike as isolated individuals lacking national traditions and a sense of cultural history. As an alternative, she advocated the remembrance of one's people, or race, through family and national *rituals. (*See* biological racism.) She acknowledged the influence of both Ludwig *Feuerbach and Friedrich *Nietzsche in the development of her views, which found ready acceptance among large numbers of people.

Ludendorff, General Erich (1865-1937). German supreme commander during World War I. Ludendorff refused to accept responsibility for the German defeat in World War I and blamed Jews and socialists for the Allied victory. With his wife, Mathilda, he founded a new religion in the 1920s. *See also* Ludendorff Bewegung; Ludendorff, Mathilda.

Ludendorff, Mathilda (1877-1966). Founder of a new religion in Germany. Mathilda Ludendorff was the third daughter of Lutheran parents. She married the zoologist Gustav Adolf von Kemnitz in 1904 and received her doctorate in neurology in 1913. After her husband's death in 1916, she founded her own religion, *Gotterkenntnis* ("God-consciousness"), in 1919 and married General Erich *Ludendorff in 1925. Together they developed her religion, which became known as the *Ludendorff Bewegung. Her main work is *The Triumph of the Will to Immortality* (1921). The Ludendorffs associated Jews and *Freemasonry with an opportunistic liberalism, democracy, internationalism and mercenary economic exploitation. Following the defeat of Germany in World War II, her movement was banned, only to be revived in the 1950s as the *Bund fur Gotterkenntnis* (League for God-Consciousness). This movement was also banned in 1965 because of its antidemocratic and *anti-Semitic teachings.

M

Maclaine, Shirley (1934-). Popular actress and film star turned *mystic and New Age guru. In many ways Maclaine is the Helena *Blavatsky of the late twentieth century, using Western ideas to interpret distorted forms of *yogic religions to a mass audience. She has been influential in the promotion of the *New Age movement. Her religious beliefs are to be found in her best-selling autobiographies *Out on a Limb* (1983), *Dancing in the Light* (1985) and *It's All in the Playing* (1987).

magic. The production of effects in the world by means of invisible or supernatural causation. Magic in its religious sense (as distinguished from illusion) is action based on a belief in the efficacy of symbolic forms that perform in an automatic manner. Magical belief holds that if a *ritual is performed correctly, then the desired result will of necessity be attained. In the past magic was seen as separate from, and essentially a more primitive thought form than, religion, but recent scholarship has tended to blur the distinction between religion and magic. *See also* sorcery; witchcraft.

magician. Someone who practices *magic to produce effects in the world by means of invisible or supernatural causation. A magician in the religious sense should be distinguished from an illusionist who entertains by tricks and sleight of hand.

Mahabharata. One of the most important Indian epics in Hindu *mythology. Mahabharata is the "Great Story" that records the history of the descendants of Bharata. The epic is approximately 100,000 verses long and includes numerous subsections. The main story is clearly older than the historical text, which was compiled sometime between 400 B.C. and A.D. 400. There is no scholarly consensus as to whether the epic is based on historical events or is purely artistic invention. The central theme develops from the myths of Vishnu's *avatars. The goddess Earth is oppressed by *demons and overpopulation and in danger of being submerged in the ocean. To relieve her, the gods take human form and descend to earth, headed by Vishnu, who is born as

*Krishna and who declares the theology of the epic in the Bhagavad Gita. The story then focuses on the history of the dynasty and its response to crisis over four generations. The epic has found its way into numerous traditional and new religious movements.

Maharishi Mahesh Yogi (1911-). Founder of Transcendental Meditation. He is said to have rediscovered the original effectiveness of *yoga in 1957 and started to teach *Transcendental Meditation in 1959. He became a popular figure in 1968, when the Beatles visited him in India, and in 1971 he established the Maharishi International University in Fairfield, Iowa. His teachings blend science, *pseudoscience, *meditation and *yogic religion. In addition to Transcendental Meditation and his university, he has founded a host of related programs.

Mahdi. The "Guided One," or messianic imam, in the *Shiah. This term is used in a general sense within Islam to refer to an awaited descendant of Muhammad who will restore the purity of Islam.

Makiguchi, Tsunesaburo (1871-1944). Founder of Soka Gakkai. Makiguchi was an elementary school principal who was deeply interested in human values and in teaching them. His writings were published posthumously as *Kachiron*, which formed the intellectual basis of the *Soka Gakkai movement. He and some of his followers were imprisoned in 1943 for not paying homage at a *Shinto shrine, and he died in prison.

mandala. A symbolic form that involves symmetrically arranged circles within larger concentric circles. It is used in *ritual and *meditation by devotees of *tantra in the Hindu tradition and Buddhism.

mantra. An "instrument of thought" in Hindu and Buddhist *meditation. A mantra takes the form of a properly repeated hymn or sound believed to have the ability to invoke the presence of a particular divinity or create a religious state.

Martin, Walter (1928-1989). Christian apologist and cult watcher. More than anyone else, Martin has shaped popular Christian attitudes to contemporary religions through his many books, particularly his best-selling *The Kingdom of the Cults* (1965; 30th edition, 1997), which has sold millions of copies. Martin's approach was essentially theological and *countercult, with a tinge of *anticult rhetoric. He had a penchant for ad hominem arguments that sought to discredit the founders of various new religions by pointing out their moral failure. *See also* cult.

Masonic lodge. Meeting place of Freemasons. Freemasons are members of an international organization who swear an oath of secrecy. The origins of the movement probably lie in twelfth-century Europe. Today the Masons are a service club. *See also* Freemasonry.

Mayans. An ancient civilization of Mexico. Many *occult writers link the growth of Mayan civilization and of ancient Egyptian civilization to a common source, such as *Atlantis. In fact, Mayan civilization developed centuries after the decline of ancient Egypt and never attained the technological skills of the Egyptians.

meditation. A religious practice found in the *yogic and *Abramic traditions that involves many different techniques to attain an exalted spiritual state. This state is often described as communion with the divine or (in the case of Buddhism) the transdivine.

Melton, John Gordon (1942-). Researcher of *new religious movements. Melton is a United Methodist minister and professor of religious studies who describes himself as an evangelical Christian. He is the author of numerous books that take a sympathetic approach to new religions and is the editor of several major encyclopedic dictionaries documenting the beliefs and practices of new religions worldwide. His critics claim that he is too sympathetic toward new religions and accuse him of being an apologist for cults. (*See* cult; cult apologist.) To this he responds that, unless one understands a religion, it is impossible to criticize its beliefs. Therefore he sees his task as promoting understanding, leaving criticism to others.

merit. An important concept in *Buddhism that counteracts the effects of *karma and can be acquired by *meditation and through acts of charity or devotion. Merit can be transferred to and from one's ancestors and other beings, thus promoting welfare in this life and ensuring spiritual progress beyond the grave or *rebirth in the western paradise. The doctrine plays an important role in the development of Mahayana Buddhism, where the *bodhisattva accrues merit that is transferred to the devotee.

Mesmer, Franz Anton (1734-1815). Physician and founder of mesmerism. Mesmer completed his study of medicine in Vienna, where he wrote his doctor's thesis on the influence of the planets on human health. He took Paris by storm in 1778, when he announced a radical new cure for numerous illnesses involving hypnotism. Later, disillusionment set in and his views became the subject of ridicule.

mesmerism. Hypnosis. Mesmerism takes its name from its founding figure, Franz Anton *Mesmer, and was an ecstatic, pseudoreligious movement that swept Europe in the late eighteenth century. Many future founders of new religions, such as Mary Baker *Eddy and Helena

*Blavatsky, were strongly influenced by Mesmer's teachings and example.

metempsychosis. Transmigration of the soul from one body to another in a cyclic life pattern. As a religious philosophy, metempsychosis appears to have originated in India around 600 B.C. and was taught by Pythagoreans in Greece, where it entered the *Orphic mysteries and both Platonism and Neo-Platonism. In India it is found in the Hindu tradition and *Jainism but not in Buddhism, where the doctrine of *reincarnation is similar but in important respects different. Some modern writers have attempted to find the idea in such Christian thinkers as Clement of Alexandria and Origen, but the supposed discovery rests on dubious assumptions and questionable readings of their works. The doctrine does, however, emerge in the works of Emanuel *Swedenborg and Annie *Besant. *See also* transmigration.

millenarian movements. Generally, any religious movements that hope for a salvation that is (1) collective, to be enjoyed by all the faithful as a group; (2) terrestrial, to be realized on this earth; (3) imminent, to come soon and suddenly; (4) total, to transform life on earth completely; and (5) miraculous, to be brought about by, or with the help of, supernatural agencies. *See also* apocalypticism; chiliasm; millennialism.

millennialism. The belief in a thousand-year period (millennium) in which the kingdom of God is to flourish and prosper. It is synonymous with *chiliasm. Millennialists tend to fall into three camps: (l) those who believe that the millennium will follow the parousia, or second coming of Christ (premillennialism); (2) those who believe that the millennium will precede the parousia of Christ (postmillennialism); and (3) those who believe that the millennium is symbolic and to be understood in spiritual terms as the reign of Christ. *See also* apocalypticism; millenarian movements.

Miller, William (1782-1849). Baptist religious leader and founder of *adventism in America. After a surprising conversion from *deism, Miller's study of the Bible led him to concentrate on the prophetic books and eventually declare that Christ would return around 1843. When this did not happen, the date was rescheduled, and further disappointments followed until his death. Miller explained his failures in terms of human error and possible mistranslations of the Bible. Miller's work led to the growth of several *millenarian groups, the most important being *Seventh-day Adventism. *See also* millennialism.

miracle. An unusual event that is seen as a significant and divine intervention in human affairs. Miracles are believed to confirm the spiritual power and authority of a teacher or religious leader, and claims to miraculous powers exist in most religious traditions. The reality of miracles came under strong attack from *deism and *Enlightenment philosophy, in which a miracle was defined as an event that broke the laws of nature and was, by definition, impossible.

modern, modernism, modernity, modernization. Various terms having to do with what is new, or the modern age. The most important of these are the following: (1) *Modern*—that which is new, as opposed to that which is ancient, and that which is innovative, as opposed to that which is traditional. (2) *Modernism*—an explicit and self-conscious commitment to the modern in intellectual, cultural and theological affairs. (3) *Modernization*—a program committed to remaking society, the political order and theological beliefs in support of the new. (4) *Modernity*—the quality and condition of being modern. All religious traditions have experienced the effects of modernity, although these have been most noticeable in Christianity, where they have been associated with secularization and explicit attacks on traditional beliefs and values in the name of science.

monism. (1) A metaphysical theory that there is one fundamental reality, of which all other beings are attributes or modes, if they are real at all; (2) the belief that there is one unifying force in the universe from which all else is derived. In the latter sense Christianity can be understood as a form of monism because everything is in some sense ultimately attributed to God.

Monist League. A *scientific religious society. It was founded in 1880 by Ernst *Haekel to promote the views of Charles *Darwin and a new nonsupernatural spirituality.

monotheism. The belief in one—and only one—God, who is both personal and transcendent. Monotheism is to be contrasted with *deism, *pantheism and *polytheism.

Moon, Sun Myung (1920-). Korean founder and prophetic leader of the *Unification Church. Moon's followers are popularly known as "Moonies." *The Divine Principle* (1973) is his major work.

Mormons. The name given to members of the Church of Jesus Christ of Latter-day Saints. The church was founded by Joseph *Smith in 1830. Mormons claim to represent true Christianity, which has been "restored" on earth through the ministry of Smith (who was called a *prophet) after centuries of apostasy. Although they are in some respects increasingly similar to traditional Christianity, the Mormons are characterized by their doctrine of continuous *revelation, which has allowed them to add *The Book of Mormon, The Pearl of Great Price* and *Doctrine and Covenants* to the Bible as well as maintain the authority of their living prophet. Among their various distinctive doctrines is the belief that God has a human body and the law of *eternal progression, which states that believers eventually become gods.

Mu. A land similar to *Atlantis or *Lemuria. The Englishman James *Churchward argued that Mu once existed in the middle of the Pacific Ocean.

Muhammad (571-632). The founder of *Islam and the last and greatest prophet according to its teaching. Through him the Qur'an was recited and written down by his followers. After initial rejection and persecution in Mecca in 622, he built a loyal following and a powerful army in Medina, and returned to Mecca in triumph in 630.

Muhammad, Elijah (1897-1975). The St. Paul of the *Nation of Islam. Elijah Muhammad organized and led the group after the disappearance of Wallace *Fard. He was a dynamic speaker and able administrator who created a major new African-American religion with its roots in Islam.

Murray, Margaret (1862-1963). Egyptologist. Murray was the author of several books, including *The Witch Cult in Western Europe* (1921), which promoted the view that an ancient pre-Christian religion, identified with witches, survived in Western Europe until at least the seventeenth century, when it was destroyed by Puritan persecution. Although accepted for a while by some scholars, this view is now totally discredited. (See Ronald Hutton, *The Triumph of the Moon* [1999].)

Murti, Ananda (1921-1990). Founder of Ananda Marga. Born Prabhat Ranjan Sarkar, he established the Hindu *revitalization movement *Ananda Marga and is believed to be a god by his followers.

mystic. Someone who claims to know God immediately through a form of spiritual inwardness, as over against knowing through sensation or ratiocination (that is, through logical processes). *See also* mysticism.

mysticism. The implications of this word are often unclear. In the study of religion it refers to the immediate experience of a sacred-human relationship, and in particular to the experiences of oneness with a divine or transdivine being or state. It is difficult to study and describe because *mystics tend to claim that their experience is self-authenticating and that it is ineffable (not capable of being satisfactorily expressed in words).

myth. A type of narrative that seeks to express in imaginative form a belief about humanity, the world and God or gods that cannot adequately be expressed in propositions. But since this word is used in both contemporary scientific and theological literature, any single definition is somewhat arbitrary. In common language *myth* is used to denote stories that have no basis in fact. This meaning is too loose for anthropologists and philosophers. Myths can be contrasted with *legends, fairy tales and so on. This implies no judgment on the truth of the story; indeed, it is possible to have a true story serve as a myth. Critics of myth argue that it tends to open the door to irrationalism. Myth has been held to be a truer or deeper version of reality than secular history, realistic description or scientific explanation can afford. This view ranges from irrationalism and post-Christian supernaturalism to more sophisticated accounts in which myths are held to be fundamental expressions of certain properties of the human mind. In biblical studies the use of the term *myth* has had a long, complex and often crude history dating from the nineteenth century. Probably the best definition is to say that a myth is a story with culturally formative power that functions to direct the life and thought of individuals and groups or societies.

N

Nag Hammadi library. A collection of Gnostic manuscripts discovered in 1945 at Nag Hammadi in upper Egypt. The texts are Coptic translations of Greek Gnostic and hermetic texts and are dated to the fourth century A.D., with the original Greek texts being dated to the second and third centuries A.D. They include the Gospel of Thomas and are our main source of direct information about *Gnosticism. As with many other ancient texts, numerous new religious and *New Age groups seek to identify with the Gnostics and use these ancient texts to "prove" that they belong to an ancient religious tradition.

Naganuma, Myoko (1899-1957). One of the founders of *Rissho Koseikai. With Nikkyo *Niwano, she founded this Buddhist *revitalization movement in 1938. She was an energetic woman who played the role of *shaman to this important *new religious movement in Japan.

Nanak (1469-1539). First Sikh guru and chief founder of the Sikh community. (*See* Sikhism.) Born a Muslim, Nanak was influenced by *Sufism and *bhakti from the Hindu tradition. He became a wandering teacher and began to preach the unity of God, whom he taught is formlessness. He referred to God as Sat Kartar (the True Creator) and Sat Nam (the True Name). Rejecting the caste system, he sought to reconcile Hinduism and Islam while reforming Indian society.

Nation of Islam. African American *new religion. Founded in 1930 by Wallace *Fard and organized by Elijah *Muhammad, this is one of the major Islamic new religions that has great appeal among black Americans. The group has become increasingly orthodox in its Islamic beliefs and has reached out to embrace the Muslim world. Today it is a fast-growing movement with an impressive record of social action among American blacks. The most famous member of the movement was Malcolm X, who was assassinated in 1965. Today the group is led by the charismatic and controversial Minister Louis X. Farrakhan (1933-).

nature spirits. Spirit beings believed to be responsible for the welfare of crops, rain, trees and other features of the natural order. Many of these spirits have the names of Greek, Celtic or Norse gods, such as Pan. Belief in such beings is sometimes mistakenly called *animism. The *neopagan movement and the *Findhorn Community revived belief in these spirits in the 1960s.

Nazism. The National Socialist German Workers Party, originally founded in 1919 and eventually controlled by Adolf Hitler. Ideologically, the party promoted a form of *fascism, but it is perhaps more accurately seen as a modern *millenarian movement. Throughout its history the Nazi Party expressed strong religious sentiments utilizing *ritual and *myth to promote its evil view of a Jewish world conspiracy and the need to destroy Judaism. Contrary to the usual Hollywood image of the jackbooted thug, the Nazi movement was led by highly educated intellectuals, many of whom had Ph.D.s from good universities, and was strongly supported by the German academic community, which was the first major social group to throw its weight behind the movement. As Peter F. *Drucker pointed out in *The End of Economic Man* (1939), the Nazis thrived on the spiritual confusion of the times, finding spiritual enlightenment in the works of Friedrich *Nietzsche and theories of *myth developed by Houston Stewart *Chamberlain, Alfred *Rosenberg and other like-minded intellectuals. Although Adolf Hitler (1889-1945) consolidated his power through political scheming and the use of force, many National Socialist intellectuals, such as Jakob Wilhelm *Hauer, believed that if the movement were to succeed, a cultural revolution first needed to displace Christianity as the religion of the people. Since 1945 this view has grown in popularity through the works of thinkers like Sigrid *Hunke and Pierre *Krebs, who have called for the creation of a new paganism. (See James M.

Rhodes, *The Hitler Movement* [1980].)

necromancy. Evoking the dead in *divination rituals.

Needleman, Jacob (1934-). American professor of religion. One of the earliest commentators on and defenders of *new religious movements, he appears to be committed to a form of spirituality associated with George *Gurdjieff (1872-1949) and is sympathetic to *Theosophy. He is the author of *The New Religions* (1970).

neopaganism. Various *new religions, including *Wicca, Celtic and Germanic religions and modern *shamanism. Traditionally a *pagan was a non-Christian, but today the term positively describes a variety of groups who purportedly revive pre-Christian religions. Neopagans have developed their own rituals and annual holidays, including celebrations of the soltices and equinoxes. They are usually *polytheistic, often feeling an affinity for *nature spirits. They are essentially a decentralized movement that rejects external authorities and controlling scriptures, vesting authority instead in the individual. They often worship a goddess and god who are equally important in their *rituals.

Nettles, Bonnie Lu (1927-1985). Cofounder of Heaven's Gate. Known to her followers as "Ti" or "Peep," she was cofounder with Marshall *Applewhite of the *Heaven's Gate movement, which committed mass suicide in 1997. She was a nurse and member of the *Theosophical Society who introduced Applewhite to theosophical teachings and other *occult influences before abandoning her work and family to become an itinerant preacher of *UFO beliefs.

New Age movement. A general term applied to a consensus of thought that arose in the 1970s and gained notoriety in the 1980s involving various types of mystical *occultism and elements of *yogic and *Abramic religions and philosophies. It began as a self-conscious movement with the 1971 publication the *East-West Journal* and found its most forceful advocate in Shirley *Maclaine. Since the mid-1990s many prominent leaders of the movement have either pronounced its "death" or distanced themselves from its more extreme expressions. Others have pointed out that *movement* is an inappropriate term for what is essentially a loose consensus of ideas and small movements.

New Church. A religious organization founded by the followers of Emanuel *Swedenborg. The group is very small but surprisingly influential in *occult circles.

new religions, new religious movements. A descriptively neutral term for new religious groups. Various religious groups that appeared during the 1970s and 1980s, such as the *Hare Krishna movement and the

*Unification Church, were quickly identified as *cults, implying that they were socially dangerous and that their members were *brainwashed. To avoid such a judgmental term as *cults,* many scholars (particularly sociologists of religion) adopted the more neutral term "new religious movements." This term was intended to prevent people from prejudging the authenticity of such groups and to serve as a way of recognizing that many of the people in these movements are motivated by genuine spiritual concerns. *See also* religion.

New Thought. A movement incorporating ideas from *Christian Science, *Theosophy and the teachings of Emanuel *Swedenborg. The movement was founded by Emma Curtis Hopkins (1849-1925) after she was excommunicated from Christian Science in 1885.

Nichiren Buddhism. A Japanese Mahayana Buddhist *sect. It traces its origin to the thirteenth-century Buddhist priest Nichiren, who sought to restore what he saw as *orthodox Buddhism. Members of this religious family stress that (1) the Buddha is eternal; (2) his personal enlightenment guarantees the *enlightenment of all sentient beings; (3) the Lotus Sutra was given by the Buddha to replace all other teachings; and (4) Nichiren is the incarnation of a *bodhisattva through whose suffering his followers may attain salvation.

Nichiren, Shoshu (1222-1282). Japanese Buddhist priest and founder of *Nichiren Buddhism. When he was twelve his family placed him under the care of the Seichoji Temple of the Tendai *sect. Later he journeyed to Mount Hiei, near Kyoto, where he pursued his studies of the sutras. But he was driven out of Mount Hiei because of his radicalism and moved on to Mount Koya to study the *esoteric teachings of *Shingon. He finally came to the conviction that the only true faith was taught by *Daishi, who had introduced *Tendai Buddhism to Japan and taught the superiority of the Lotus Sutra over all other sutras.

Nietzsche, Friedrich Wilhelm (1844-1900). German philosopher. Nietzsche was influenced by Ludwig *Feuerbach, who profoundly influenced modern thought by his radical rejection of Christianity and the Western intellectual tradition. In *The Gay Science* (1887) Nietzche told the parable of the madman, which contains the prophetic phrase "God is dead" to describe the condition of modern life. Rejecting the mob, he advocated a heroic ethic that despised women and looked for the coming of the "superman." A brilliant essayist, his work critiques *modernity and provides the basis for many new religions, such as those associated with Jakob *Hauer, Mathilda *Ludendorff, Carl *Jung and *Bhagwhan Sri Rajneesh.

nirvana. A complex *Sanskrit term that expresses the ideal in Buddhism. Its meaning is "blowing out" or "cooling" and is called Nibbana in *Pali. Western writers sometimes describe it as annihilation, although Buddhists often deny that this is the meaning. Nirvana is correctly described as "the unconditioned," which means that because everything we experience is conditioned, we cannot really know the true nature of nirvana, although by *meditation we may experience it. The term is used loosely in many new religions.

Niwano, Nikkyo (1906-1999). Cofounder of Rissho Koseikai. Niwano joined the Reiyukai, a *Nichiren Buddhist movement, where he was introduced to the Lotus Sutra and to the group-counseling practice called Hozo. Eventually he became dissatisfied with the attitude of the leader toward the Lotus Sutra and, together with Myoko *Naganuma, formed a new organization called *Rissho Koseikai, one of the leading *new religions of Japan.

nondualism. An Indian philosophical system that rejects dualism. It is characteristic of the work of thinkers like *Sankara and of the *Vedanta, and often mistakenly labeled *monism by Western writers unfamiliar with Indian philosophy.

Norman, Ernest L. (1904-1971) and Ruth E. (1900-1993). Founders of a *UFO religion. Ernest (an electrical engineer) visited a psychic convention in Los Angeles and subsequently, in 1954, cofounded with his wife the *Unarius Academy of Science in El Cajon, California. (Unarius stands for Universal Articulate Interdimensional Understanding.) Ruth, known as the Archangel Uriel, became the principal medium of the movement, which was influenced by Helena *Blavatsky's *theosophical thought. The Unarius Library consists of over 125 volumes, much of it written by the Normans, who professed to receive messages from aliens through channeling.

Nova Religio. The main North American academic journal dealing with *new religious movements.

Noyes, John Humphrey (1811-1886). Religious and social reformer who developed perfectionist and *adventist views. Noyes was converted through the revivals in New York State and was studying for the ministry at Yale when he pronounced himself "sinless" in 1834. This was based on the belief that Jesus had returned in A.D. 70 and inaugurated a new age. He subsequently established two communes, one in Putney, Vermont (1840-1848), and one in Oneida, New York (1848-1881), where his ideas of perfectionism, biblical communism, complex marriage, male continence, population control, mutual criticism and education were practiced and promulgated. In 1876 he emigrated to Niagara Falls, Ontario. Noyes was the author of *History of American Socialism* (1870) and other works. *See also* Oneida.

numinous. A term coined by Rudolf *Otto to evoke the feeling or sense of the *holy, which he viewed as fascinating, fearful and beyond rational analysis.

nuns. Female religious devotees living in communities devoted to the service of the group. They are usually celibate. The earliest evidence for the institution comes from Buddhism, and from there the practice seems to have spread to Hinduism and eventually to Christianity.

O

occult, occultism. Modern terms used to describe a wide spectrum of beliefs usually connected with some supposedly secret tradition. Occult practices often involve ritual *magic and various forms of *spiritualism. The root meaning is "hidden" or "that which is hidden," implying the need for initiation into a secret or closely guarded spiritual tradition. In recent years many occult ideas have merged in the *New Age movement.

Oneida Community. A perfectionist religious community founded by John Humphrey *Noyes in 1848. Noyes founded the community on the basis of a Christian communism that entailed a belief in human perfectibility. Believing that sin was rooted in selfishness, the Oneida members shared all things, including spouses in an arrangement called "complex marriage." The community disbanded in 1880 when its profitable manufacturing industries became a joint stock company.

oracles. Various devices or deities used or consulted to foretell the future. Sometimes oracles are distinct from *divination; in other cases they are part of elaborate divination *rituals.

Order of the Golden Dawn. A secret, ritual-magic society (also known as the Hermetic Order of the Golden Dawn) founded in London in 1888 by three Rosicrucian Masons. (*See* Freemasony; Rosicrucians.) The society fragmented into four separate groups in 1909. It played a key role in promoting modern *neopaganism and ritual *magic.

Origen (185-254). Early church father. Origen was one of the earliest Christian thinkers to attempt to reconcile Christianity with Greek philosophy, and in his interpretation of the Bible he employed *allegory. He also taught that human souls preexist before they are born but vigorously denied *reincarnation and related doctrines. Today many

*New Age-type groups illegitimately appeal to Origen as a source for their views.

Orphism. A Greek mystery religion centered on the god Orpheus and associated with the *Eleusinian mysteries, which featured *rebirth as one of their central beliefs.

orthodoxy. Any religious movement or set of beliefs that belongs to the mainstream of a religious tradition and preserves that tradition's core teachings; true or right beliefs. It contrasts itself with *heresy, or deviation from the historical tradition of a particular faith.

Osho movement. *New religion founded by *Bhagwan Sri Rajneesh in 1953. It is based on a psychological technique called "dynamic meditation" and blends ideas from numerous other religious traditions without endorsing any. A highly successful movement, it lacks clear beliefs other than the criticism of other faiths and liberal beliefs about sexual freedom.

Otto, Rudolf D. G. (1869-1937). German theologian who pioneered the phenomenology of religion. Otto's *Idea of the Holy* (1923; revised edition, 1929) sets out the thesis that *religion is essentially the apprehension of the *numinous, or wholly other, which humans grasp through religious insight.

P

pagan. Traditionally a person in the Greco-Roman world who was not a Christian. Later the term came to be applied to all non-Christians.

Paine, Thomas (1737-1809). Deist and American revolutionary figure. Born in England of Quaker parents, Paine immigrated in 1774 to America, where he became a leading propagandist in the American Revolution. His books *Common Sense* (1776) and *The Rights of Man* (1791-1792) stand as passionate appeals for democratic republicanism, while *The Age of Reason* (part one, 1794; part two, 1796), written in a French revolutionary prison, is a devastating attack on religious belief. A much-neglected thinker, Paine anticipated modern criticisms of religion, including those of Ludwig *Feuerbach (1804-1872), Karl Marx (1818-1883) and Sigmund *Freud (1856-1939). His *skepticism influenced people from Joseph *Smith (1805-1844) to Methodist Sunday school teachers in England who lost faith as a result of reading his books. A careful reading of his work shows that he also promoted a *religion of nature that lent itself to the development of *neopaganism. (See Jack Fruchtman Jr., *Thomas Paine and the Religion of Nature* [1993].)

Pali. The ancient language of the canonical texts of *Theravadan Buddhism that was preserved in Ceylon (Sri Lanka), Burma, Thailand, Laos and Cambodia.

Pandurang, Atam Ram (1823-1898). Founder of *Prarthana Samaj and one of the leaders of the Hindu renaissance in the late nineteenth century.

panentheism. A view combining insights of *pantheism and *deism by arguing that the world is included in God's being on the analogy of cells within a larger organism. This view was systematically and philosophically elaborated by Alfred North Whitehead (1861-1947) and applied to theology by Charles Hartshorne (1897-2000).

pantheism. The doctrine that all things and beings are modes, attributes or appearances of a single, unified reality or being. Hence nature and God are believed to be identical. Although the term is often incorrectly used to describe Hindu thought and various other *yogic religions, it appears to accurately describe many *new religious movements and the views of most *New Age thinkers.

paradigm. A popular *esoteric and confusing term used in many different and undefined ways by Thomas Kuhn in his book *The Structure of Scientific Revolutions* (1962) to signify "what members of a scientific community share." It is commonly taken to mean "a coherent system of concepts that confers order on the whole field of knowledge or a segment of it belonging to a particular scientific discipline." Kuhn's usage legitimates relativism in many fields, although he denies that his view is relativistic.

People's Temple. A congregation led by Jim *Jones. The People's Temple was a congregation of a mainline and theologically liberal Protestant denomination, the Disciples of Christ, and was led by the charismatic figure Jim Jones. Widely praised for its social action programs and its radical political stance, the congregation under Jones's leadership founded a socialist settlement at Jonestown, Guyana, in 1977. Following a mass suicide on November 18, 1978, the group was labeled a *cult by the media and became a key element in the American *anticult movement.

peyote cult. A religious *revitalization movement that swept through various North American native groups in the late nineteenth century. It survives today as a religious movement that combines traditional practices and beliefs with others derived from Christianity. The central sacrament of the *cult is the use of mescaline from the peyote cactus as a hallucinogenic drug.

phallus cults. Various religious movements have worshiped the phallus, giving strong religious significance to sexuality. The practice is common in the Hindu tradition and is rationalized as the recognition of creative energies. It is distinctive of the worship of Siva. *See also* Saivism.

pilgrimage. The practice of visiting sacred sites imbued with historical or other significance within a given religious tradition. In many new religions, places like *Glastonbury are centers of pilgrimage.

Plato (c. 427-347 B.C.). Greek philosopher. Plato held that the material and sensible world is merely a temporary copy of permanent, unchanging Forms, which are the object of all real knowledge. True ethical values are attained only by those individuals who have the proper perspective of soul or mind and who place reason above the baser elements of their personality. The best government is possible only when philosophers, who are rational members of the state, become rulers. His teacher was Socrates, and Aristotle was his pupil—together they are the three greatest ancient Greek philosophers.

Platt, Parley P. (1805-1859). Early Mormon evangelist and theologian. (*See* Mormons.) Platt's creative speculation about the law of *eternal progression in his classic *The Key to Theology* (1855) sought to harmonize modern science and religion.

Plotinus (205-270). The originator of Neo-Platonist thought. Neo-Platonism was the dominant philosophy in the Greco-Roman world until the sixth century and had a great impact on the development of both theology and *mysticism. He is the author of *The Enneads*.

polytheism. Belief in a plurality of gods, as opposed to *monotheism, which is a belief in only one God.

positive thinking. A distinctly American movement originating in the nineteenth century that believes in progress and stresses the role of thought in the creation of material well-being. It has influenced many religious groups, from *Christian Science to the Word of Faith movement.

possession. The state or experience of being possessed or taken over by a spirit being. *See also* demons; exorcism.

Prabhupada, Swami A. C. Bhaktivedanta (1896-1977). Founder and guru of the *Hare Krishna movement. A successful businessman, Prabhupada left his family to become a monk when he was fifty-eight years old. After extensive study, in 1965, at the age of seventy, he felt called to spread "Krishna consciousness" in America. For the rest of his life, he worked ceaselessly to establish the Hare Krishna movement and spread Hindu *bhakti practices in the West.

Prarthana Samaj. Hindu reform movement. The name means "Prayers Society," and it was founded in 1867 by Atam Ram *Pandurang, who was strongly influenced by Christian missionary thinking. It proclaimed a monotheistic message and sought to modernize Hindu society.

primal experiences. Fundamental spiritual experiences that shatter preconceived notions about the rational order of the universe and material nature of existence. These experiences involve dreams, *visions, encounters with ghosts or spirits, precognition and even *visions of Jesus.

proleptic experience. A life-changing, revelatory experience that profoundly affects an individual's assumptions and view of the world and is ascribed to the work of God, a spiritual being or a supernatural force.

prophecy. The act of *revelation whereby a prophet gives an inspired message from God or the gods. Usually prophecy is associated with foretelling the future, but it can also include messages of inspiration or admonishment that reveal the will of God toward a particular people or even an individual.

prophet. A person, male or female, who foretells the future or delivers inspired, divine messages. Sometimes prophets use *divination and special devices to obtain their messages; on other occasions they speak as directly inspired.

Prophet, Elizabeth Clare (1939-). Shamanistic leader of a *new religious movement. (*See* shamanism.) The Summit Lighthouse, a spiritualist-type new religious movement, was established in 1958 by her late husband, Mark L. Prophet. Elizabeth was attracted to the movement and they married in 1963. After her husband's death in 1973, she became the leader of the movement. She claims to have received more than 1,800 "dictations" from *ascended masters, archangels and other advanced spiritual beings. The group's headquarters is in Gardiner, Montana.

pseudoscience. The practice of such things as *pyramidology and *trance channeling, as well as belief in UFOs, ancient astronauts and so on, on the basis of supposed scientific evidence that is in fact nonsensical. Pseudoscience uses scientific-sounding terminology but totally lacks scientific support. Ignoring systematic investigation and scientific methodology, it is usually openly hostile to modern science.

Pure Land Buddhism. East Asian Mahayana Buddhist *sects that emphasize faith in Amida Buddha. (*See* Jodo.) They express this faith through *meditation and the recitation of his name as a means of attaining *rebirth in the western paradise, or *Pure Land.

pyramid texts. Ancient Egyptian religious texts written in hieroglyphics on the inner walls of pyramids dealing with funeral rites, *rituals, *magic spells, prayers and other issues affecting the dead. They are cited by some modern *occult writers. *See also* Egyptian religions.

pyramidology. A modern *pseudoscience that finds special meaning in the shape of a pyramid. Pyramidology has featured in the growth of many *new religious movements, from *British Israelism to the early *Jehovah's Witnesses. The measurements of pyramids, particularly the Great Pyramid, have been used as a basis for predictions and the interpretation of *prophecy, often in conjunction with an attempt to interpret various biblical books such as Daniel. *See also* Egyptian religions.

Q

Quimby, Phineas Parkhurst (1802-1866). Healer and hypnotist. A Lebanese-born American, Quimby was a religious innovator, healer and hypnotist who formulated a "science of happiness." His work gave rise to New Thought and inspired Mary Baker *Eddy, the founder of *Christian Science.

Qumran. The site of a Jewish community that flourished between 150 B.C. and A.D. 68. In 1947 an Arab shepherd boy discovered in nearby caves the first scroll in what proved to be a unique collection of ancient Hebrew and Aramaic manuscripts known as the *Dead Sea Scrolls, which are thought to belong to the Jewish *sect known as the *Essenes.

R

Radha Soami Satsang. Hindu reform movement. It emerged after the death of Shiv Dayal (1818-1878), who incorporated Sikh beliefs and practices into a form of *yoga. The movement differentiates itself from *Sikhism in that the guru replaces the scripture as the source of religious knowledge and in that it rejects Sikh initiation.

Radhakrishnan, Sarvepalli (1888-1975). *Brahmin interpreter of Hindu traditions and Indian philosophy who became vice president of India. Radhakrishnan expounded a *universalistic version of *Vedanta that minimized the doctrine of Maya, the essential illusory nature of all things. His many books include *The Bhagavadgita* (1948), *The Hindu View of Life* (1927), *Indian Philosophy* (two volumes, 1923-1927) and *Eastern Religions in Western Thought* (1939).

Rael, Claude (1946-). *UFO religious leader. The French race car driver and journalist Claude Vorihon claimed to have an encounter with a UFO in 1973 while hiking in the mountains. He subsequently changed his name to Claude Rael and founded his own new religion, the *Raelian movement, based on what he claims is the message given to him by the aliens he met. He says that he is the last of forty *prophets sent by God to warn humans of impending doom.

Raelian movement. *UFO religion. The movement was founded in 1973 by Claude *Rael (1946-) to communicate the message of space aliens intended to save humankind from imminent destruction through atomic war. The movement is based near Montreal, in Canada's French-speaking province of Quebec, and claims over twenty thousand members worldwide. They worship a godlike being called Elohim whom they expect to arrive in a UFO sometime in the near future. As a movement, it has been particularly successful in appealing to social outcasts such as prostitutes, partly because of its unorthodox views on free sexual expression and stigmatization of marriage as the ownership of women by men.

Rama. Next to *Krishna, the most important Hindu god and the seventh *avatar of Vishnu. Rama is the supreme example of patience, faithfulness and justice. The *Ramayana saga describes his exploits.

Ramakrishna (1836-1886). One of the principal figures in the nineteenth-century Hindu renaissance. He trained in the classical traditions of Hindu *mysticism but went beyond the boundaries of Hindu spiritual practice by experiencing *enlightenment in a way that embraced both dualism and *nondualism. He married but claimed to lead a completely "renounced life," without sexual contact. His wife, Sarada, was known as the "Holy Mother" and was recognized as a saint. He abandoned traditional priestly food and taboos and spoke of his sense of identification with Jesus of Nazareth and Allah. His most prominent disciple was Swami *Vivekananda.

Ramana Maharishi (1879-1951). Commonly regarded as one of the greatest Hindu saints of the twentieth century. Ramana settled near Madras at the age of twenty and remained there until his death. He was a sage who claimed to have experienced the identity of the *Atman and *Brahman as taught by the *Vedanta tradition of Hindu philosophy.

Ramananda (13th c.). A *Brahmin who rejected the caste system to become a leading advocate of *bhakti. He sought to synthesize the Hindu
tradition and Islam and drew his closest disciples from all walks of life,
including an outcast and two women. His ideas and the movement he
founded influenced the development of the *Sikhs and several other
*sectarian groups that renounced caste and promoted *bhakti.

Ramanuja (1017-1137?). Hindu philosopher. Ramanuja taught a modified version of *monism that acknowledged God and the separate spirits of men as well as the material world, or nonspirit. The spirits of men
he regarded as essentially different from God, who is both the creator
and the material out of which the world is formed. He taught that pe-
riodically human spirits are reabsorbed into God, and he distinguished five ways or stages of worship, each being higher than the
last. He was a leading opponent of the philosopher Samkara (eighth to
ninth century), whom he attacked for moral laxity and intellectual
confusion.

Ramayana. With the *Mahabharata, one of the two great epics of Indian
literature. The Ramayana tells the story of Rama and his wife, Sita,
who is kidnapped by the demon king of Ceylon. With the help of the
Monkey King, Rama eventually slays the demon and rescues his wife,
whose loyalty Rama questions. Sita throws herself on a pyre, but the
fire god, Agni, refuses to accept her sacrifice, and Rama realizes her innocence. After he returns to his kingdom and assumes the throne, his
people again question Sita's purity, creating doubts that cause Rama
to send Sita away. She gives birth to twins and asks the earth to swal-
low her, which it does, thus finally proving her innocence. Years later
Rama recognizes the twins and gives them his kingdom, allowing him
to return to heaven as Vishnu. The epic, which is approximately 24,000
stanzas long, dates from around the first century (although sections of
it are definitely much later) and is traditionally ascribed to Valmiki. A
Hindi version that is more overtly religious, emphasizing *bhakti, was
produced in the sixteenth century by Tulsi Das (1532?-1623).

Rampa, T(uesday) Lobsang (1911-1981). Theosophical writer. Cyril
Henry Hoskins, an English plumber, disguised himself as a Tibetan lama named Lobsang Rampa and published the immensely successful
book *The Third Eye* (1957). His ruse was discovered by *News of the
World,* the tabloid that had initially serialized his book, and exposed
the fraud. Nevertheless, Rampa continued his writing career, producing over twenty books full of *theosophical teachings and his own
imaginative reinterpretation of Helena *Blavatsky's thought.

Ramtha. The ancient spirit entity who speaks through J. Z. *Knight. Ramtha first appeared in 1977 by speaking through the former fundamentalist Christian and highly successful spiritualist medium, or *trance channeler, J. Z. Knight. Ramtha claims to be a warrior from the lost continent of *Lemuria and *Atlantis, making Knight an important figure in the *New Age movement.

Rand, Ayn (1905-1982). Russian émigré and objectivist philosopher. Rand popularized her views through novels such as *The Fountainhead* (1943), *We the Living* (1935) and *Atlas Shrugged* (1975). Although neglected by most academic philosophers, her views have had an immense influence, strongly promoting the sort of individualism and libertarian political ideas that are found in some new religions. *See also* egoism.

Rastafarians. Jamaican religious *sect. The Rastafarians believe in the divinity of Ethiopian emperor Haile Selassie and refuse to accept reports of his death. The movement has political overtones and makes the smoking of marijuana a sacrament. Members of the group are accused of involvement in drug trafficking. Their distinctive hairstyle of dreadlocks became popular as a result of their music: reggae.

rebirth. A general term that can mean *reincarnation, *transmigration or some other form of *metempsychosis.

reincarnation. A technical term in Hindu and Buddhist thought associated with the doctrine of *karma and implying the continuation of consciousness after physical death but not necessarily the rebirth of a soul. In the West, however, it is usually confused with ideas of *transmigration of the soul or *rebirth through many lifetimes and is promoted by claims that people remember their past lives.

religion. A common technique of *anticult activists is to claim that many *new religions are not religions at all. Therefore a clear definition of *religion* is important for the study of new religions. Although hundreds of different definitions of *religion* exist, one of the best and most widely accepted is from Ninian *Smart's paper "Meaning in Religion and the Meaning of Religion" (1969): "a set of institutionalized rituals with a tradition and expressing or evoking sacral sentiments directed at a divine or transdivine focus seen in the context of the human phenomenological environment and at least partially described by myths or by myths and doctrines." Another useful definition is in Rodney *Stark's *Sociology* (1989): "any socially organized pattern of beliefs and practices concerning ultimate meaning that assumes the existence of the supernatural."

revelation. The act whereby God or gods disclose information to humankind. In Judaism revelation comes through the Hebrew Bible; in Christianity, through the Hebrew Bible and New Testament. In Islam the Qur'an is the only source of revelation. Hindus associate revelation with Sruti, or "what is heard," and have increasingly seen this in connection with the *Vedas, *Upanishads and other religious literature. Buddhism treats the sayings of the Buddha as a form of revelation, although it denies the involvement of God. *Jainism denies all supernatural sources of revelation. In other traditions revelation comes from ancestors and gods for specific purposes. Traditionally the *Abramic religions have claimed that revelation ended with the closing of their canon of scriptures. Claims about continuing revelation have led to *revitalization movements and religious *revivalism, which often provoke the wrath of the *orthodox, who see such claims as *heresy.

Review of Religious Research. One of the principal academic journals in the sociology of religion. It is published by the Religious Research Association and carries a number of articles on new religions.

revitalization movements. Any movement that sets out to revive a religious tradition or an attempt on the part of a previously acculturated group to regain and reaffirm early religious traditions. These movements are often syncretistic in doctrine and ceremony.

revivalism. Outbreaks of intense, often mass religious excitement that seek to revive and restore a religious tradition that is believed to be in decline. Revivalism can often take the form of a *revitalization movement.

Rg Veda. The most ancient book of the Hindu tradition. The Rg Veda consists of four collections of vedic hymns composed before 900 B.C. and preserved in oral tradition until they were written down by Hindus in the sixteenth century and later by Muslims in the eighteenth and nineteenth centuries. The hymns were used in sacrificial rituals by *Brahmins and are treated as eternally existent. There are 1,028 hymns. The most important gods referred to in these hymns are Indra, Agni, Varuna and Soma. Vishnu and Rudra are present, but only as minor deities. Many scholars see a tendency toward *monotheism in the hymns. The Rg Veda was translated into English by Max Müller and Hermann Oldenberg in the 1890s from a language that predated *Sanskrit.

Richardson, James (1941-). Scholar of new religions. (*See* new religious movements.) Richardson, an American scholar with doctorates in sociology and jurisprudence, is a professor at the University of Nevada. A strong defender of religious freedom, he has undertaken extensive sociological research into new religions and is the author of six books and over one hundred academic articles. His books include *Organized Miracles* (1979), *Money and Power in New Religions* (1988) and *The Satanism Scare* (1991).

Rinzai. Zen Buddhist sect. Founded in China in the ninth century and introduced to Japan during the twelfth century, Rinzai is one of the two most important *sects in *Zen Buddhism. It is distinguished by its seated meditation on *koan and the use of unorthodox means to attain *enlightenment.

Rissho Koseikai. Buddhist *revitalization movement. With a name translated "Association of Truth and Fellowship," this movement was founded in 1938 by Myoko *Naganuma and Nikkyo *Niwano on the basis of *Pure Land Buddhism.

ritual. Repetitive behavior that is fixed by tradition and is often a sacred custom. In the study of *religion it means traditional religious behavior or actions. Religious reformations or *revitalization movements often interpret their own reactions against the ritual expressions of another group as a total rejection of ritual.

Romanticism. A late eighteenth- and early nineteenth-century movement in art, literature, philosophy and religion that involved sentimentality, self-expression and idealized melancholy. The movement arose as a reaction to the rationalism of the *Enlightenment and stressed emotionalism, sensualism, fantasy and imagination over rational order and control. Romanticisim held that reality is found through feeling, immediate experience, spiritual illumination and the practice of brooding and listening to the inner voices. Romantics had a deep interest in the past, especially the Middle Ages, and in Nordic mythology, folklore and primitivism. They published medieval historical records and literature. The impact of Romanticism on religion and theology has been immense. In America it stimulated *Transcendentalism and an interest in Eastern religions. In Britain the Romantics played a direct role in the creation of *neopagan movements. In Germany the majority moved toward a Germanic nationalism and *völkisch religion.

Rosenberg, Alfred (1893-1945). Chief theorist of the Nazi Party who was executed following the Nuremberg trials. Rosenberg wrote extensively on religion and the need for spiritual renewal based on beliefs in *Atlantis and various *theosophical-type theories connected with the work of Helena *Blavatsky, Paul de *Lagarde, Houston *Chamberlain and Friedrich *Nietzsche. *See also* fascism; Nazism.

Rosicrucians. Esoteric religious society. The Order of the Rosy Cross was publicized in two books by Lutheran pastor Johann Valentin Andreae (1586-1654) as an ancient secret society possessing *esoteric knowledge. The idea was taken up by various thinkers, including René Descartes (1596-1650) and Johann Comenius (1592-1670), but no organization was ever discovered. In the late nineteenth century various *occult groups claiming to be Rosicrucians emerged, promoting a hodgepodge of religious ideas, including *reincarnation. Scholars do not believe that any of these groups can be linked with an ancient society.

Ross, Rick (1952-). Leading American Jewish *anticult activist. Ross maintains an extensive and sometimes useful website where he identifies himself as an "expert consultant, lecturer and intervention specialist" and "deprogrammer." He appears to be self-taught and provides no evidence that he has any formal academic expertise in the area of religious studies, sociology or psychology.

Roy, Ram Mohan (1774-1833). Founder of Brahmo Samaj. Roy was a Bengali *Brahmin, educated in English, who showed a rationalistic inclination. After studying at a Muslim institution in Patna, he accepted *monotheism. He admired the New Testament and Christian ethics but rejected Christ's divinity. Convinced that the *Upanishads taught *monotheism and were free from social abuses, in 1828 he founded the *Brahmo Samaj for the propagation of his religious and social views. He is buried in Bristol, England.

rta. The cosmic moral order that, in the *Vedas, sustains the universe.

Russell, Charles Taze (1852-1916). Founder of the movement that became *Jehovah's Witnesses. Russell grew up in a pious Congregationalist home but rejected his early beliefs after a secular conversion. He retained his love for the Bible, eventually developing his own system, which centered on the issue of prophecy. He formed his own independent congregation in 1878. Preaching that the Second Coming of Christ had occurred invisibly in 1874, he predicted the end of the world would come in 1914. Eventually his followers became known as Russellites and formed the International Bible Students' Association, which later split into a number of groups, the best known being the Jehovah's Witnesses.

Rutherford, "Judge" Joseph Franklin (1869-1942). Jehovah's Witnesses leader. Rutherford was the successor to Charles T. *Russell as leader of the Watchtower Bible and Tract Society and was the immediate founder of the *Jehovah's Witnesses. His numerous books, publications and radio broadcasts, as well as his able leadership, made the organization the world community it is today.

Ryobu-Shinto. A *syncretistic movement that sought to unify Japanese *Shinto with *Buddhism. It was suppressed during the Meiji period (1868-1912), although certain forms still prosper today.

S

Sadler, William S. (1875-1969). Founder of *Urantia. Sadler was a professor of medicine at the University of Chicago, lectured in pastoral counseling at McCormick Theological Seminary and was a prolific author. During the 1920s he was visited by a patient whose wife claimed she was kept awake by his constant chattering. In 1934 and 1935 Sadler recorded what the man said during counseling sessions in which the man was allowed to fall asleep. Sadler then published these monologues as *The Urantia Book*. Later, in 1950, he created the Urantia Foundation as a nonprofit educational endowment.

Saint-Simon, Claude Henri (1760-1825). French socialist philosopher. Saint-Simon sought to promote a new form of religion devoid of the supernatural trappings of Christianity. He strongly influenced Auguste *Comte, whose works develop Saint-Simon's program. Saint-Simon's books include *The Reorganization of European Society* (1814) and *The New Christianity* (1825).

Saivism. The worship of Siva in Hinduism. The *cult of Siva appears to have roots in the Indus Valley civilization that existed before the *Aryan invasions. In the classical Hindu tradition, two very different forms of Saivism emerged. The first gave it ideological sophistication through the *monism of *Sankara and *Vedanta, out of which a *tantric tradition also developed. The second major tradition of Saivism was a Tamil version that emphasized *bhakti and a dualistic type of *monotheism.

sangha. The order of monks in Buddhism.

Sankara (788-838). Indian Brahmin philosopher, advocate of *Vedanta and founder of several monasteries in India. He seems to have regarded Siva and Vishnu as equal manifestations of the universal spirit and taught the illusory nature of the separation of humanity from the Brahman.

Sanskrit. The classical language of India. Sanskrit became the holy language of the Hindu tradition, although the earliest Hindu scriptures, such as the *Rg Veda, and many later *bhakti texts are not actually written in it. It is also the original language of many early Buddhist texts, although most of these have been preserved in translation only.

Santeria. Caribbean religion. Santeria is a *new religion that originated during the sixteenth and seventeenth centuries in the Caribbean among slave populations from Nigeria and Benin. It has roots in traditional practices of the Yoruba. It took root, and possibly originated, in Cuba, from where it spread throughout the Caribbean to places like Brazil and (more recently) the United States. Essentially it is a *syncretistic religion that blends *African traditional religion with Roman Catholicism along with late nineteenth-century elements of European *spiritualism.

Sargant, William (1918-1988). British psychiatrist and opponent of "brainwashing." Sargant's book *The Battle for the Mind* (1957) was a sustained attack on evangelical Christian conversion as a form of *brainwashing. His work was a response to the success of the Billy Graham Crusade in England in 1951 and was critiqued by D. Martyn Lloyd-Jones (1899-1981) in his *Conversions, Psychological and Spiritual* (1959). His ideas were popularized in North America by Flo Conway and Jim Siegelman in *Snapping* (1978) and are found among members of the *anticult movement.

Sartre, Jean Paul (1905-1980). French novelist and radical nihilistic, existential philosopher. (*See* existentialism.) Sartre's novels, such as *Nausea* (1938), spoke to a generation of Europeans following World War II. A student of Martin *Heidegger, his major philosophical works are *Being and Nothingness* (1943) and *Critique of Dialectical Reason* (1960).

Satan. The devil, or personalized force of evil, who entices humankind away from the service and love of God. *See also* Satanism.

Satan, Church of. Satanist *new religious movement. The Church of Satan was founded by Anton Szandor La Vey (1930-1997) in 1966. Intensely individualistic, the Church of Satan teaches indulgence, vengeance, physical gratification and the attainment of personal power and seems to owe some of its ideas to Ayn *Rand's objectivism. *See also* Satan.

Satanism. *Esoteric religious groups and individuals who worship *Satan. They are often associated with ritual sacrifice and unconventional sexual practices. Satanic groups include the *Church of Satan and various ritual *magic organizations. Contrary to most press reports, there is no solid evidence that satanic groups sacrifice children or carry out ritual murder. Nor should Satanism be associated with *Wicca or other forms of *neopaganism, which strongly disassociate themselves from satanic rituals, beliefs and practices.

schismogenesis. A term coined by anthropologist Gregory Bateson to denote the social and psychological state that leads to conversion or other drastic personality changes.

Schleiermacher, Friedrich Daniel Ernst (1768-1834). German Protestant theologian and founder of modern liberal theology. Schleiermacher rose to fame following the publication of his *Speeches on Religion to Its Cultural Despisers* (1799), in which he defines religion as the "feeling" or "sense" of absolute dependence and separates the study of religion from science and other academic disciplines. Many of the founders of new religions in Germany, such as Jakob *Hauer, were inspired by his work.

Schopenhauer, Arthur (1788-1860). The first modern philosopher to draw upon Indian philosophy for inspiration. Deeply pessimistic, Schopenhauer embraced the concept of maya (illusion as an explanation of reality) and rejected all appeals to history as a basis for philosophy. A scathing critic of G. W. F. Hegel (1770-1831), whom he saw as a pedestrian lackey of Prussia, he developed a concept of the will that influenced such thinkers as Friedrich *Nietzsche and Sigmund *Freud. He saw women as the servants of men. His major work is *The World as Will and Idea* (1819).

Schucman, Helen (1909-1981). Occult figure. Schucman was an American psychologist who became an *occult writer and medium and the author of *A Course in Miracles* (1975).

Schuon, Frithjof (1907-1998). Popular modern spiritual writer. Schuon was a member of the *traditionalist school of philosophy whose *Castes and Races* (1982) is a sophisticated defense of racism. His books include *The Transcendent Unity of Religions* (1984).

scientific pantheism. A *new religion that claims to promote religious diversity and tolerance. Founded in 1995 by Paul *Harrison (1945-), it is similar to *neopaganism in that it emphasizes nature without a belief in individual spirits; rather, all of the cosmos is divine. In this sense it is somewhat like Ernst *Haekel's *Monist League.

scientific religion. A *new religion claiming to be based on purely scientific principles and thus setting religion on a new and realistic base. Examples are Ernst *Haekel's *Monist League, various forms of *positive thinking, *scientific pantheism and *Scientology.

Scientology. A controversial therapy based on a *new religious movement founded by L. Ron *Hubbard. Scientology aims at applying religious philosophy to recover spirituality and to increase individual ability. Originally called *dianetics, it maintains that the human mind is capable of resolving any and all problems through humans becoming their own savior and freeing their inner spiritual being, or Theatan. Scientology is a *scientific religion that promotes a Westernized version of *yogic religion supported by the rich mythology found in Hubbard's science fiction novels. In many respects Hubbard was a modern *shaman. Although many attempts have been made to deny the religious nature of Scientology, it has too many features of actual religions to be dismissed as a pious fraud or secular philosophy.

sect. A term often loosely used to mean a religious group that has broken away from an older tradition. Confusion is created by the fact that it is sometimes used theologically to refer to groups of questionable *orthodoxy or outright *heresy. Sociologically the term has been contrasted with *church and used of groups that live in tension with the surrounding society. In his book *Sociology* (1989) Rodney *Stark defines a sect as "religious bodies in a relatively high state of tension with their environment but which remain within the conventional religious tradition(s) of their society."

seer. Someone credited with the gift of *prophecy or second sight. Belief in seers is found in all cultures and may be understood in religious or secular terms.

Self-Realization Fellowship. Hindu *revitalization movement. It was founded in 1920 by Paramahansa *Yogananda and has its headquarters in Los Angeles. It teaches a form of *Vedanta adapted for Western consumption through references to the teachings of Jesus and biblical figures and texts, and it promotes its own form of *yoga.

Seventh-day Adventists. Adventist denomination. The name was adopted in 1861 by a group that arose out of the Millerite movement, a *revitalization movement that expected the imminent return of Christ. They observe the Sabbath and certain food laws based on the Old Testament (*vegetarianism and avoidance of tea, coffee and alcohol). Unlike most *millenarian movements, they emphasize education and have an impressive record of medical work. Although some Christians accuse them of *heresy, they are now essentially orthodox and evangelical in their theology and are a dynamic and fast-growing denomination with extensive missionary programs. *See also* adventism; Miller, William.

Shah, Idris (1924-1996). Popular writer and Sufi teacher. Shah's books, which include *The Sufis* (1964), have sold over fifteen million copies and have had a major impact on the growth of new forms of spirituality in the West. Shah's work has been appreciated by authors like Doris Lessing (1919-) and Robert *Graves (1895-1985).

Shakers. *Millenarian communal society. Originating in a Quaker revival meeting in 1747, the Shakers were a group of people distinguished by their physical shaking during worship. They came under the leadership of "Mother" Ann *Lee, who was recognized as a female Christ. She immigrated to America with her followers in 1774, where they established several Shaker communities. The Shakers were a utopian group, known for their austere, utilitarian architecture and furnishings and their practice of celibacy and communal living. Among their many achievements was the invention of the washing machine. Only a handful of Shakers remain today.

shaman. A word of northern Asiatic origin that means "priest" or "medicine man." It is used of individuals who communicate with the spirit world after entering an ecstatic state often brought on by rhythmic drumming and frenzied dancing.

shamanism. An indigenous religion of northern Eurasia in which a central feature is trance and the control of spirits by exceptional individuals, or *shamans, who negotiate between this world and the spirit world. Shamanism is found among hunting peoples and presupposes a belief in a multiplicity of spirits and the survival of the soul after death. As a coherent religious system, it is practically extinct, although a revival of interest in shamanism has occurred in various *new religious movements, including the *Unification Church and (in a certain sense) *Scientology.

shell shock. A term originating from the trench warfare of World War I, when many soldiers became mental wrecks as a result of their being subjected to continuous artillery bombardment. The term forms the basis of William *Sargant's theory of *brainwashing.

Shembe, Amos (1907-1996). Ama-Nazarite leader. (*See* Ama-Nazaretha.) Amos Shembe was a younger son of Isaia *Shembe and leader of the largest branch of the Zulu Ama-Nazarite movement, which split into two rival factions after the death of Johannes Galilee *Shembe. Under the leadership of Amos, the group moved in a more orthodox Christian direction, with a greater emphasis given to the Bible and the person of Jesus.

Shembe, Isaia (1867-1935). Founder of the Ama-Nazarites. (*See* Ama-Nazaretha.) Isaia Shembe was a Zulu healer and visionary who was baptized (1906) in the African National Baptist Church and then formed the Nazirite Baptist Church (1911). He then became the founder of the Ama-Nazarites, the largest independent religious movement among the Zulus. (*See* African independent churches.) Regarded as God by many of his own people, Isaia Shembe is usually spoken of as a *prophet by Europeans. But this designation was vigorously denied by his son Amos and grandson Londa. His writings and sayings have been translated by Londa *Shembe as *The Prayers and Writings of the Servant of Sorrows Thumekile Isaiah Shembe,* making them the first scriptures of a new religious movement in Africa to appear in English.

Shembe, Johannes Galilee (1904-1975). Ama-Nazarite leader. (*See* Ama-Nazaretha.) Johannes Galilee Shembe was the successor of Isaia *Shembe. Under his able leadership, the Ama-Nazarites were the second largest independent religious movement in southern Africa and the most important among the Zulu.

Shembe, Londa Nsi Kayakho (1944-1989). Leader of a smaller and more progressive branch of the Ama-Nazarites. (*See* Ama-Nazaretha.) He called himself the Third Shembe, thus identifying his work and personality with that of his grandfather Isaia *Shembe. He strongly rejected the idea that the Ama-Nazarites were simply a form of Africanized Christianity, insisting instead that they were an African religion in their own right, with distinct doctrines, some of which he believed were similar to those found in Judaism and the Hindu tradition. He was assassinated on April 7, 1989.

Shembe, Vimbeni (1945-). Leader of the Ama-Nazarites who succeeded his father, Amos *Shembe, in 1996 and has ably led the church through a time of social transition. *See also* Ama-Nazaretha.

Shiah (Shiites). The smaller of the two major divisions in Islam. The Shiah, or followers of Muhammad's son-in-law Ali, believe that the spiritual and temporal headship of Islam should reside with the descendants of the prophet. They are the dominant group in Iran and Iraq.

Shingon. Mystical and syncretistic Japanese Buddhist religious movement. (*See* mysticism; syncretism.) Founded in 806 by Kobo *Daishi, Shingon incorporates the gods and even *demons from other religious traditions within its *mythology. They are seen as manifestations of the Buddha, whose body is the entire cosmos. Shingon is distinguished by its use of the *mandala, or diagram representing the vitality and potentiality of the universe.

Shinran (1173-1262). Japanese Buddhist scholar and reformer. Shinran founded Jodo Shinshu, the "True Pure Land Faith." (*See* Jodo; Pure Land Buddhism.) He studied *Tendai Buddhism at Mount Hiei before leaving to follow *Honen, the priest who founded the Jodo sect. Shinran developed a more radical doctrine that emphasized the importance of faith rather than the number of recitations of religious formulas. He advocated the marriage of monks and sought to minimize the gulf between clergy and laity.

Shinshukyo. An *esoteric *Shinto religious movement. It was founded by Yoshimura Masamochi (1839-1915) in 1882 to restore Shinto *orthodoxy and promote divine healing. Its best-known rites are a fire walking ceremony and bodily purification using boiling water.

shintai. A sacred object in a *Shinto temple in which the spirit of a deity is believed to reside.

Shinto. The way of Kami, or the gods, which is the traditional religion of Japan and central to Japanese culture and national identity. It is based on prehistoric religious practices, a priesthood and household rites. In modern Shinto, until the end of World War II, both the emperor and the physical lands of Japan were considered divine. The status of the emperor today is uncertain, and scholars question whether the *deification of the emperor is an integral part of the religion or a development that took place in recent times.

Shupe, Anson (1948-). American sociologist. Shupe was coauthor, with David *Bromley, of *The Moonies in America* (1979) and *The New Vigilantes: Deprogramming, Anti-Cultists and New Religions* (1980). These works gained both authors the enduring hatred of *anticult activists, who immediately labeled them *cult apologists.

Shushi school. The *orthodox school of Japanese Confucianism. It was introduced by *Zen monks in the fourteenth century and adopted by the Tokugawa Shogunate as the official system of Japanese morality.

Sikhism. A religion that synthesizes Islam and the Hindu tradition. Sikhism grew out of various Indian movements that sought unity between the best in the Islamic tradition and the best in the Hindu tradition. This movement crystallized in the work of Nanak (1469-1539), the first of ten gurus who created and led the Sikh community. Nanak preached the unity of God and taught the centrality of *bhakti-type devotion, using the repetition of the divine name. Sikhs repudiated the caste system and banned images from worship.

skepticism. The belief that the possibilities of knowledge are severely limited and that truth is difficult if not impossible to attain. Skeptical theories may promote an abandonment of the search for certainty and the adoption of systematic doubt.

skeptics. The name given to certain philosophers who doubt the adequacy of the senses and reason to furnish reliable knowledge about the nature of things. They advocate withholding assent and the suspension of judgment.

Smart, Ninian (1927-2001). Scottish philosopher and scholar of religions. Smart introduced religious studies to British universities and pioneered the teaching of world religions in English schools. His works include *Reasons and Faiths* (1958), *Doctrine and Argument in Indian Philosophy* (1964) and *The World's Religions* (1989) as well as the popular television series *Long Search*. Smart's work is important because he defined key religious terms before the rise of *cult controversies that clouded the issues, and he can therefore be trusted for his definitions.

Smith, Huston (1919-). Interpreter of world religions. Born of missionary parents in Soochow, China, Smith became one of the most popular writers on comparative religion in America through the publication of his 1958 book *The World's Religions* and 1997 film series shown on public television. Influenced by the *traditionalist school of thinkers, he is a strong advocate of what he calls the "world's wisdom traditions," which he sees as preaching a deeply rooted spirituality shared by all truly religious people.

Smith, Joseph (1805-1844). American visionary and founder of Mormonism. (*See* Mormons.) Smith claimed to have begun receiving spiritual visions in 1820, and as a result of the religious confusion created by competing *sects he published *The Book of Mormon* (1830). He said he discovered the book with the help of an *angel and translated it with God's assistance from reformed Egyptian hieroglyphics written on golden plates. On April 6, 1830, he founded the Church of Jesus Christ of Latter-day Saints. Teaching the importance of continuing *revelation, he subsequently published *Doctrine and Covenants* (1835) and *The Pearl of Great Price* (1851), which, together with *The Book of Mormon,* provide the basis for the church's doctrine and organization. Opposition to the practice of polygamy, which he began openly teaching in 1843, led to his arrest and murder by a mob in 1844.

Smuts, Jan Christian (1870-1950). South African prime minister, army general, statesman and philosopher. Smuts's work *Holism and Evolution* (1926) is credited by many as being an early statement of the philosophy of the *New Age movement.

snake handling. An exotic religious practice of handling deadly vipers.

The practice emerged among Appalachian Pentecostal groups in the early twentieth century. The practice is based on Mark 16:17-18, which speaks of "taking up serpents." Snake handlers interpret these verses literally and see snake handling as a sign of faith.

Soka Gakkai. A Japanese *new religious movement. It was founded in 1930 by Tsunesaburo *Makiguchi and Josei *Toda as a lay association of Buddhists and is based on the teachings of *Nicheren and the *Lotus Sutra. The group maintains a television ministry and a major temple complex. Originally its involvement with political issues created considerable hostility, but this has moderated in recent years.

Solar Temple. A *New Age-type *occult group whose members were involved in a murder-suicide on October 5, 1994.

Solomon's Wisdom. An *occult text used by the *Theosophist Helena *Blavatsky. The exact nature of this work is unclear. There is an *apocryphal Jewish text called Wisdom of Solomon and a number of occult works with similar titles.

soma. A plant regarded as divine in vedic Hinduism, soma is mentioned in vedic literature and was valued for its hallucinogenic powers by *Brahmins, who used it in rituals.

sorcery. The exercise of ritual *magic with evil intent and often involving the use of physical objects, spells, potions and poisons. *See also* witchcraft.

soul. The immortal element in human beings sometimes regarded as our true self. The existence of the soul is denied in Buddhism and certain Hindu traditions. Other Hindu philosophies teach the existence of the soul as integral to the notion of *transmigration.

Southcott, Joanna (1750-1814). English *mystic. At the age of forty-two, Southcott claimed to hear the voice of God. She declared herself a *prophet and the bride of Revelation 19 and proclaimed the end of the world. She began to practice automatic writing, and in 1800 she published six pamphlets recording her views and prophecies. This led to the formation of a small but influential group of followers. Many of her prophecies have been promoted by *occult groups and recently by some members of the *New Age movement.

Spangler, David (1945-). A spiritual writer and *New Age thinker who became leader of the *Findhorn Community in the 1980s.

Spencer, Herbert (1820-1903). English positivist philosopher, sociologist and liberal. Spencer was the dominant English intellectual figure in the latter half of the nineteenth century. Applying Charles *Darwin's views to society, he developed a philosophy of progress expressed in his *First Principles* (1862) and greatly contributed to the development of anthropology and sociology. His ambitious *Principles of Sociology* (three volumes, 1876-1896) can be seen as a forerunner of general systems theory because of his insistence on the self-regulating nature of social systems. Zealously he looked for a new *scientific religion that would supersede Christianity.

Spengler, Oswald (1880-1936). German historian and philosopher. Spengler's influential work *The Decline of the West* (1914-1922) helped set the tone for modern intellectual pessimism and *existentialist philosophy. His work has influenced the thinking of many founders of new religions because of his rejection of objectivity and his belief that Western society was coming to an end.

spiritism. A mode of thought and, more importantly, behavior, based on the belief that the spirits of the dead and other spirits interact and sometimes even communicate with the living. Such intercourse normally takes place through dreams, illness and unusual events, which reveal the presence of a spirit. When the spirit disturbs the living, a *shaman or similar religious expert is called upon to solve the problem and, if appropriate, the shaman directly contacts the spirit or spirits concerned. Appeasement of the spirit often involves sacrifice and *rituals that appear similar to group therapy.

spirits. Disembodied entities that display the characteristics of individual persons and are sometimes regarded as the *souls of dead ancestors. In most religions spirits are regarded as potentially dangerous and often as evil.

Spiritual Counterfeits Project (SCP). The leading Christian ministry to address the issue of new religions during the 1970s and early 1980s. It was founded in 1973 by Brookes Alexander and David Fetcho. In 1975 the group won a major court case against *Transcendental Meditation, claiming that it was actually a religion and therefore not entitled to funding from the American government. During the 1980s, SCP was almost destroyed by a punitive lawsuit brought by members of *Local Church, who claimed that it and its leaders were libeled in SCP publications. This lawsuit forced SCP to declare a form of bankruptcy and led to a period of decline, which was halted in the 1990s by extensive reorganization under the leadership of Tal Brooks. SCP publishes a regular newsletter, *Spiritual Counterfeits Journal,* and several books, in addition to maintaining a website.

spiritual healing. The belief that through prayer or other spiritual exercises an individual may be healed physically or psychologically. Such healing often involves the intervention of someone who is regarded as having a gift of healing or who is seen as being a saint.

spiritualism. A modern form of *spiritism. Spiritualism dates from 1848, when two teenage sisters, Margaretta and Katie Fox, of Hydesville, New York, reported hearing rappings in their home. They interpreted these noises as messages from a peddler who had died in the house. Enthusiasm for spiritualism swept North America and spread to Europe and Latin America. The teachings of Emanuel *Swedenborg, bitter rivalry among competing Christian denominations and a growing awareness of the problems of *biblical criticism, as presented by *deists like Thomas *Paine, may be seen as contributing factors to the growth of the spiritualist movement. After rapid growth in the 1850s, when (according to some estimates) as many as 75 percent of Americans visited spiritualists, enthusiasm declined. Spiritualist ideas have had an influence far greater than the number of committed spiritualists would suggest, making an important contribution to the growth of *new religious movements. In places like Brazil, spiritualism has encouraged the growth of *syncretism among Roman Catholic, traditional African and Native American religious traditions.

Starhawk (1951-). Neopagan leader and author. A Jewish-American originally named Miriam Simons, Starhawk is leader of the *neopagan movement and calls herself an ecofeminist and peace activist. She is a prolific writer whose books include *The Spiral Dance: A Rebirth of the Religion of the Great Goddess* (1979). She seems to accept unquestioningly Margaret *Murray's thesis.

Stark, Rodney (1940-). Sociologist of religion. Stark is regarded by many as the leading American sociologist of religion. His many books include *The Future of Religion* (1985), which he wrote with William Sims Bainbridge as a study of new religions.

Steiner, Rudolf (1861-1925). Austrian theosophist. Steiner was founder of *anthroposophy and the Waldorf School movement. Strongly influenced by Johann Wolfgang von *Goethe, Steiner promoted a form of Christian *theosophy that emphasized aesthetics and various healing techniques, including *homeopathy.

Stonehenge. A circle of standing stones in southern England, the purpose of which is unknown, although it was probably used in some kind of religious *ritual. Popular imagination has associated the building of Stonehenge with the *druids, but this is totally false. Today Stonehenge is an inspiration to various *neopagan groups.

Strauss, David Friedrich (1808-1874). Radical German theologian and one of the founders of *biblical criticism. Strauss lost his early Christian faith after visiting a *spiritualist medium. His book *The Life of Jesus* (1835) caused a storm by its denial of the supernatural, which he attributed to *myth. Strauss sought to reinterpret the Bible in secular terms devoid of any supernatural explanation. His work inspired Mathilda *Ludendorff and various other founders of new religions, such as Annie *Besant.

Subud. Javanese *new religion. Subud was founded by a Javanese seeker, R. M. Muhammad Subhu *Sumohadiwidjojo, sometime in the 1930s. Its teachings were transmitted to the Western world in the 1950s and accepted by John G. *Bennett, who until then had promoted the teachings of George *Gurdjieff. Essentially, Subud teaches a form of *meditation, the *latihan,* based on a semipantheistic view of God's relationship to the world. The movement appears to be an offshoot of Islam that incorporates traditional Javanese religious concepts of *yogic origin. The name Subud stands for "Susila, Budhi and Dharma," and the movement's leaders claim that it is "not a new religion nor a sect of any religion, nor is it a teaching" but rather is a "symbol" for the right way of living. Despite these disclaimers, it displays all the characteristics of a religion and has to be judged a *new religious movement by scholars.

Sufism. Islamic mystical movement. The name is derived from the Arabic word for wool and reflects the fact that early Sufis wore coarse woollen clothing in protest against what they saw as the decadence of the caliphate in the seventh and eighth centuries. The movement emphasizes love of God and has been traced to Christian influences by some scholars, although today most authorities think it reflects a genuine flowering of indigenous spirituality within Islam. By far the most important Sufi scholar known to the West is al-Ghazali. (*See* Ghazali, al-.) In medieval Islam, Sufis formed a number of great Sufi orders that imposed a disciplined way of life on their members but did not require celibacy. In time these orders became a major force in Islamic missionary activity and the revitalization of Muslim society. Beginning in the twelfth century, various Neo-Platonic ideas began to influence the Sufi movement, the theology of which became increasingly *pantheistic. By the nineteenth century, the Sufi orders dominated society in the Islamic world. They suffered a major setback in the twentieth century through the rise of secular nationalism in Muslim countries, many of which, like Turkey, banned the orders. Today they appear to be flourishing, embracing wide segments of Muslim society and adapting to *modernity. Many *new religious movements embrace aspects of *Sufism through spiritual teachers like Frithjof *Schuon, René *Guénon and Kahlil *Gibran, who claim to be Sufi initiates, while writers like Huston *Smith and Ken *Wilber promote Westernized versions of Sufi ideas.

Sumohadiwidjojo, R. M. Muhammad Subhu (1901-1987). Javanese religious teacher who founded the Subud Brotherhood in the 1930s.

Sunni. The majority party in Islam, distinguished by its rejection of the claims of Ali. The name comes from the practice of finding solutions to problems not discussed in the Qur'an by appealing to the sunna (customs) of Muhammad in Medina and to the Hadith, traditions concerning the life of Muhammad. This is in contrast to the *Shiah, who believe in the authority of inspired imams.

Suzuki, Daisetsu Teitaro (1870-1966). Buddhist scholar. Suzuki was a Japanese scholar who popularized Buddhism in the West through his writings on *Zen. His first book was a Japanese translation of Emanuel *Swedenborg's *Heaven and Hell* (1910), while his later writings, including *Mysticism, Christian and Buddhist* (1957), display a firm grip on Western thought, leading him to grapple with the problem of interreligious communication. He traveled widely and in 1921 married an American professor of Buddhism at Kyoto University. He began the publication of the magazine *Eastern Buddhist,* which he also edited. He is perhaps best known for his book *Zen and Japanese Culture* (1959). Suzuki was closely associated with both the *Bollingen Foundation and the *Eranos Seminar.

Swami Dayananda Saraswati (1824-1883). Founder of a Hindu reform movement. In 1870 he founded *Arya Samaj, a reform movement that, among other things, embraces *monotheism and rejects the worship of images. Later he founded several other movements, such as the Cow Protection Society in 1882. He was born into a *Saivite family in a predominantly *Jain town and eventually made it his mission to modernize the Hindu tradition.

swastika. Ancient Hindu symbol of a broken cross. It signifies Vishnu and the evolution of the cosmos and was believed to be a symbol bringing success. It was adopted for its *occult significance by the German National Socialists in 1919 as a sign of good luck. *See also* Nazism.

Swedenborg, Emanuel (1688-1772). Swedish scientist, philosopher, theologian and *mystic. Swedenborg's ideas strongly influenced *Romanticism and are in many ways the inspiration for the *New Age movement and have influenced many other religious groups, including *Mormonism and the *Unification Church. After a brilliant engineering career, Swedenborg experienced strange dreams and visions, leading to a religious crisis between 1743 and 1745. This culminated in a *vision of Christ and in Swedenborg's religious conversion. Renouncing science, he spent the rest of his life propagating his new ideas and founded the *New Church, known as the New Jerusalem Church, or Swedenborgian movement.

syncretism. The combining of teachings, practices and doctrines from different and apparently contradictory religious traditions to create a new interpretation of an existing tradition or a *new religious movement.

Syzygy. A short-lived academic journal on new religions that was published in the early 1990s.

T

Tagore, Rabindranath (1861-1941). Bengali writer and poet whose book *The Religions of Man* (1931) expresses a broad Hindu humanism.

tantra. A Hindu term that originally referred to sacred texts in both the Hindu and Buddhist traditions. It came to be understood as a means of attaining *enlightenment through the use of *magic and *rituals of a sexual nature.

tantric Buddhism. That branch of Buddhism that developed *tantra as an *esoteric system involving *magic and sexual practices believed to overcome desire by overindulgence.

tao. A central concept for both Confucian and Taoist thought meaning "the Way." The tao signifies the course of action, or road, people ought to follow in life. It is the basic principle of the entire universe. *See also* Taoism.

Tao Te Ching. The main philosophical text and foundation of *Taoism. It combines philosophical speculation with *mystical reflection. The meaning of its title is "The Tao: Its Virtue and Power," and it is ascribed to Lao-tzu. It was written about 250 B.C. as a polemic against Confucianism and realist philosophies and contains many poems.

Tao Tsang. The canon of *Taoism. It contains over 1,120 books, the date and authorship of which are generally unknown. They use *esoteric language and were first collected around 745 B.C. for use by initiates.

Taoism. An indigenous Chinese religion. Taoism grew out of earlier *shamanism and *magical cults that were joined with mystical elements in the philosophy of Lao-tzu and Chuang-tzu. It originally aimed at the realization of perfect happiness and the prolongation of life through unity with the *tao by practicing nonactivity, noninterference and humility while renouncing force, pride and self-assertion. The techniques used included *alchemy, asceticism, health and dietary rules, a Chinese form of *yoga, *magic, petitionary prayer, and the worship of powerful deities.

Tendai Buddhism. The leading Japanese school of Buddhism. It was founded by Dengyo *Daishi in 805 on the basis of the Lotus Sutra and was centered on the monastery at Mount Hiei near Kyoto. It teaches that the historical Buddha was a manifestation of the eternal Buddha nature, which is the fundamental essence of the universe. As a result, the Buddha becomes an object of faith enabling individuals to realize their own ultimate Buddha nature and thus attain *enlightenment.

Theosophical Society. A society that promotes comparative religion, *magic and *esoteric *mysticism. It was founded in 1875 in New York City by the famous Russian *spiritualist Helena *Blavatsky (1831-1891) and by Henry Olcott (1832-1907). In 1878 the founders moved to India, where they established the international headquarters of the movement. After their death, their British convert, the former freethinker Annie *Besant, became the movement's leader. This change of leadership led to the promotion of Jiddu *Krishnamurti as the new Avatar. When he rejected this role and repudiated Theosophy, the movement suffered a blow from which it has scarcely recovered. Nevertheless it remains important today because of its influence on the growth of Indian nationalism, individuals like Gandhi, the *counterculture of the 1960s and the *New Age movement.

Theosophy. Mystical tradition propagated by the *Theosophical Society. Theosophy is a form of *monism, which teaches spiritual *evolution and seeks reality through *mystical experience based on finding *esoteric meanings in the sacred writings of the world.

Theravadan Buddhism. The main rival to Mahayana Buddhism and the dominant religion of Sri Lanka, Burma, Thailand and Cambodia. It is known as the "Lesser Vehicle" because of its strict interpretation of the Buddhist canon and its emphasis on the monastic order, the *sangha. The movement arose in the fourth century B.C. as a result of controversy over the role of the laity. It claims to preserve the authentic teachings of the Buddha and to be the oldest and purest form of Buddhism. The Theravadan tradition began to take shape with the second Buddhist Council in 250 B.C. but took its classical form between the fifth and tenth centuries A.D. During the nineteenth century, when Buddhism was first encountered by the West, it was this tradition that at first gained recognition because of its apparent rationality and supposed modern rejection of the supernatural.

Thoreau, Henry David (1817-1862). American *Transcendentalist philosopher. Thoreau's reflections on self-sufficiency in his book *Walden* (1854) and his thoughts on faith have greatly influenced *positive thinking.

Thule-Seminar. A leading neofascist group. (*See* fascism.) The Thule-Seminar promotes the idea of cultural revolution as a precursor to political change and sees religion as a key factor in social change. Recommending people to return to the religion of their ancient ancestors, the group is strongly anti-Christian. The main spokesperson is the French philosopher and cultural critic Pierre *Krebs (1943-), who wrote his doctorate on German composer Richard *Wagner. It maintains a significant Internet presence.

Tibetan Buddhism. After the failure of Buddhism in India during the twelfth century, Tibetan monks became the main inheritors of the Indian Buddhist tradition, preserving many ancient documents and practices that were rejected by *Theravadan Buddhism in the South. From Tibet, Buddhism spread to China, Korea and Japan, where the Mahayana tradition flourished to produce *Pure Land, *Zen and a host of other schools. In Tibet itself a theocratic government was established and *tantra flourished. Tibetan Buddhism, which is sometimes called Lamaism, spread to the West in the 1950s following the Chinese communist invasion of Tibet.

T'ien-T'ai. An influential branch of Chinese Buddhism. Founded in the sixth century by Chih-i (538-597), it based its teachings on the Lotus Sutra and the teachings of Nagarjuna, who emphasized the totality of being, thus identifying the parts with the whole. It declined as a result of persecution in the ninth century, but not before it had spread its message to Korea and Japan, where it is known as *Tendai Buddhism.

Tnevnoc cult. Using the standard characteristics of a "cult" identified by the *anticult movement, David *Bromley and Anson *Shupe analyzed the dangers of the Tnevnoc cult in a brilliant article published in *Sociological Analysis* (volume 40, 1980). They concentrated on such things as isolation from the world, restricted diets and sexual practices. They then explained that "Tnevnoc" is "Convent" spelled backward and that they were actually applying the anticult criteria to Roman Catholic orders to show that the criteria are unreliable. *See also* cult; new religious movements.

Toda, Josei (1900-1951). Cofounder of *Soka Gakkai.

traditionalist school. A group of loosely related philosophers and religious teachers who were inspired by the works and teachings of René
*Guénon. The traditionalist school included such well-known figures
as Julius *Evola, Frithjof *Schuon, Mircea *Eliade, Ananda *Coomaraswamy and, as a fringe member, Joseph *Campbell. Many members
of the school, such as Evola, were self-confessed and unrepentant fas-
cists who identified *fascism with a higher form of spirituality. The
school takes its name from the idea that civilization arises from a "tradition" identified with a unified primordial or perennial philosophy
that lies behind the outward expressions of all major religious faiths.
Thus all religions are ways to God or the divine and of equal value
once one discovers their underlying unity. Harsh critics of the *modern world, the leading traditionalists saw fascism as a politicized form
of spirituality that sought to renew spiritual values in defiance of *Enlightenment rationality. *See also* Nazism; *völkisch* thought.

trance channeling. A modern variation of *spiritualism or mediumship
that is translated into *pseudoscientific terminology. It involves a
"channeler," or medium, communicating a message from a spirit being, an extraterrestrial or an ancient or ascended master.

Transcendental Meditation (TM). Hindu-based *new religious movement. TM was the first really successful new religious movement of the
1960s. It emerged from the Hindu tradition as a therapy-type group of-
fering psychological well-being. The founder, *Maharishi Mahesh Yogi
(1911-), denied that TM was a religion. This enabled his movement to
appeal to a wide spectrum of people who might otherwise have ignored
his teachings and to apply for U.S. government funding and other forms
of assistance. Taken to court in 1978, TM was found to be a religion under the terms of American law. It teaches a simplified form of *yoga and
practices initiation with *occult overtones using *mantras in *Sanskrit
that invoke various Hindu deities.

Transcendentalism. An American Romantic movement. This religious
movement grew out of *Unitarianism in the 1830s and became one of
the nineteenth century's most influential *new religions. It is associated with Ralph Waldo *Emerson and Henry David *Thoreau but has intellectual roots in German *Romanticism and writers like Johann
Wolfgang von *Goethe, who preached extreme individualism, liberalism and a *pantheistic view of God. Promoting *mysticism and an interest in *yogic religions, Transcendentalism contributed to the rise of
many modern *new religious movements in the nineteenth century.

transmigration. A form of *metempsychosis or *rebirth teaching that at death the soul leaves the body to be reborn in another body as a baby. It is closely associated with, and often confused with, *reincarnation.

U

UFO religions. Religions based on contact with space aliens who visit earth in Unidentified Flying Objects (UFOs). Since the publication of George *Adamski's *Flying Saucers have Landed* (1953), numerous new religions have developed, all of which claim to be based on contact, real or telepathic, between their founder or founders and the occupants of UFOs. These are usually said to be the spacecraft of an advanced civilization. Two of the most successful of these are the *Aetherius Society, founded by George *King, and the *Raelian Movement founded by Claude *Rael. Other more infamous UFO groups include the *Heaven's Gate Community and the *Solar Temple.

Unarius Academy of Science. A *UFO religion. It was founded by Ernest L. and Ruth E. *Norman in 1954 as a vehicle for communicating messages of redemption and the salvation of earth from higher beings located on Venus. This is a UFO contactee group with its own scriptures based on writing of the Normans and other leaders. They practice forms of *meditation, have *theosophical ideas and await the coming of a super race known as the Pleiadeans. (Unarius is an acronym for Universal Articulate Interdimensional Understanding.)

unconscious. A psychological concept popularized by Sigmund *Freud and Carl *Jung, who argued that below the conscious, rational aspect of the mind there lies a realm that has the ability to affect our dreams, thoughts and actions without our being consciously aware of the source exerting the influence on us. Many other scholars see this as an unproved assumption that is part of modern irrationalism.

Unification Church. Korean *new religious movement. The Unification Church is a controversial movement that gained much publicity in the 1970s. The full name of the movement is the Holy Spirit Association for the Unification of World Christianity, and it was founded in 1954 by an engineer named Sun Myung *Moon. The principal document of the movement is *The Divine Principle* (1973), which lays out its fundamental teachings. The theology of the church is one of the most comprehensive found in any of the new religious movements. It consists of a systematic attempt to interpret the Bible from the perspective of Korean thought based on Confucian and Buddhist philosophy with insights gained from Korean *shamanism. The result is one of the most comprehensive efforts yet to produce an intellectually defensible non-Western theological system based on the Bible. Among the many ideas generated by this theology (those that are likely to influence similar non-Western theologies in the future) are Indemnity, the Fourfold Position, the idea of the Principle, and the Lord of the Second Advent. The Unification Church publishes the academic journal *Dialogue and Alliance* and numerous books on its own theology and practices. Between 1994 and 1999 the movement underwent numerous rapid transitions, during which time *Moon announced that the cycles of providence that guided the activities of the church had come to an end, necessitating its transition from a church to the Family Federation for World Peace. He also transferred the focus of his attention from North America to South America.

Unitarianism. A modern religious movement characterized by its rejection of the doctrines of the Trinity and the deity of Christ. It first appeared in Poland and Hungary among Anabaptists during the Protestant Reformation but remained dormant until 1785 and the birth of the first American Unitarian congregation in Boston. The theology quickly spread among Congregational churches in eastern Massachusetts and found support at Harvard Divinity School, which became its center. Unitarianism is a creedless, rationalist movement that rejects orthodox Christian views about the authority of the Bible and stresses instead many forms of divine *revelation and the inherent goodness of humanity.

Universal Life. Theosophical movement. Originating in Germany as *Universelles Leben*, the group was founded by Gabriele Witek (1933-), who acts as God's *prophet. This is a *theosophical-type group similar to *New Thought. The group spread to North America in the 1990s.

universalism. A theological view within Christianity holding that all people will eventually be saved, as opposed to the traditional *orthodox position maintaining that only people who show repentance and faith in Christ will obtain salvation.

Upanishads. Hindu scriptures. The term means literally "to sit near" or "near sitting," and it can refer to a secret, a *mystical doctrine or teaching or, most commonly, the collection of texts that since the eighth century B.C. has been known as "the last of the Vedas." (*See* Veda.) The content and doctrine of the Upanishads vary considerably—from treatises that promote *atheism to devotional theism. Thus they represent a wide spectrum of philosophical schools and outlooks. The thirteen

classical Upanishads were composed between the eighth and fourth
centuries B.C., but many later works also use the name, some of which
are dated as late as the fifteenth century.

Urantia Brotherhood. Theosophist movement. This movement (also
called the Urantia Fellowship) was founded by Dr. William S. *Sadler
after he received messages from a spirit being that were mediated to
him through one of his patients when the man fell asleep. The movement is based on these revelations as found in the 2,000-page text of
the *Urantia Book,* according to which Urantia is the ancient name of the
earth. The teachings of the group are clearly influenced by *Theosophy
and Helena *Blavatsky and James *Churchward's views of lost civilizations.

V

Vaisnavism. The cult of Vishnu that emphasizes *bhakti and the worship of gods like *Krishna. It is credited with producing the *Bhagavad-Gita and an extensive devotional literature rich in *myth and
symbolism. Its chief rival in the Hindu tradition is *Saivism, which
arose around the same period of time, 300 B.C. to A.D. 300.

van Baalen, Jan (1889-1968). Christian cult watcher. Van Baalen was a
Christian Reformed pastor who in 1938 published a best-selling book,
The Chaos of Cults: A Study in Present-day Isms. This book remained in
print until the mid-1980s, and more than any other work, it defined the
meaning of the word *cult* for the general Christian public. (*See* cult.)
His approach to new religions was strictly theological, involving a
thorough critique of their beliefs from the viewpoint of Christian *orthodoxy.

Varuna. A god in Hindu scriptures who first appears in the early *Vedas
as a sky god, later to become the all-seeing deity.

Veda. Literally "knowledge," signifying the sacred knowledge or *revelation that has been "heard," according to the Hindu religious tradition. It began as oral tradition and became a written tradition only
much later. The Vedas are ancient revelations found in a series of
hymns, ritual texts and speculations composed over a period of a millennium, beginning around 1400 B.C. The earliest extant documents
are probably from around the fifteenth century and were recorded by
Muslim authors.

Vedanta. One of the six classical schools of Hindu philosophy and the
one that is best known in the West. The name literally means "the end

of the Veda." (*See* Veda.) It is based on the *Upanishads and interprets the ritual practices of the Vedas in terms of symbolic meanings. There are three main schools of Vedanta: (1) Advaita, which promotes *monism; (2) Viaiadvaita, or qualified *nondualism; and (3) Dvaita, which is a form of dualism. All three are similar to Platonism in aiming to go beyond the limits of empirical observation to explore the nature of *Brahman. Both Sankara and *Ramanuja taught forms of Vedanta even though they presented sharply differing interpretations of the tradition. In the late nineteenth century various thinkers sought to create a synthesis between various aspects of Vedanta and Western forms of idealism, while Swami *Vivekananda, Sarvepalli *Radhakrishnan and Sri *Aurobindo adapted Vedanta to the theory of *evolution and Western science.

vegetarianism. The refusal to eat meat. This is often justified on religious grounds derived from *yogic religion.

Vinaya-Pitaka. The first of three sacred books of Buddhist scriptures. It is principally concerned with questions of discipline and the rules of monastic life.

visions. A revealed understanding of ultimate reality or the nature of God commonly claimed by the founders or practitioners of *new religious movements. Conversion to specific new religious movements often follows a vision that the believer interprets as a sign confirming the truth of the teachings of the movement.

visions of Jesus. A form of *primal experience that is surprisingly common and that does not necessarily lead to conversion to Christianity. Empirical evidence suggests that comparatively large numbers of people report encounters with Jesus. In some cases these visions lead to Christian conversion; in other cases people join new religions or found their own; while in still other cases people are deeply moved but do not allow the vision to affect their life. (See Phillip H. Wiebe, *Visions of Jesus* [1997].)

Vivekananda, Swami (1863-1902). Indian religious leader and philosopher who successfully introduced the teachings of *Vedanta to the West. After becoming a *skeptic as a result of reading modern philosophy, he was converted to Hinduism by *Ramakrishna in 1881. Vivekananda argued that the Hindu tradition united science and spirituality in ways that overcome rationalist criticisms of Christianity. In 1897 his speech at the World Parliament of Religions in Chicago was a great success, launching him into a career as the first Hindu guru to captivate Western disciples.

völkisch **thought.** A fascist-type worldview. It is an unsatisfactory term for what Armin Mohler called "the conservative revolution." Later Mohler admitted that he meant his term to be a synonym of **fascism*— a term he felt was unusable following World War II. Julius *Evola and other *traditionalist thinkers share this distinct type of thinking, which some of them also identify with fascism. *Völkisch* thought involves an emphasis on the importance of *mythology, communalism, the importance of elite thinkers, a rejection of historic Judeo-Christian ideas and a strong dislike of democracy and Americanism. The term *völkisch* is derived from *völk* ("folk" or "people") but has emotional and intellectual connotations that are virtually untranslatable.

W

Wagner, Richard (1813-1883). German composer. Wagner's operatic works promoted *neopagan myths. He was a rabid *anti-Semite and advocate of a pure German religion. (See Paul Lawrence Rose, *Revolutionary Antisemitism* [1990].)

Wahhabiya. A *revitalization movement in Islam originating in the eighteenth century. The movement owes its origin to Muhammad 'Abd al-Wahhab (1703-1792), who denounced idolatry, including visiting the tombs of saints, invoking *prophets, saints and *angels and seeking their intercession, and making vows to anyone but God. It stresses predestination and denounces *allegorical interpretation of the Qur'an. Demanding that faith should be proved by works, followers of al-Wahhab made attendance at public prayer obligatory, forbade use of the rosary and stripped mosques of ornaments. In 1902 Ibn Sa'ad captured Riyadh and the holy cities of Mecca and Medina, then later, in 1925, established a Wahhabi dynasty in Arabia. Although puritanical, the movement is modernizing and has no hesitation about using the results of Western science.

Weber, Max (1864-1920). German sociologist. Weber's influential works, including *The Protestant Ethic and the Spirit of Capitalism* (1920), did much to promote the sociology of religion. His important contributions include the use of ideal types, discussions of *charisma and his Protestant ethic thesis, which is often referred to as the "Weber thesis."

Weltanschauung. German philosophical term referring to an overarching perspective that shapes how one looks at the world, its people and problems. A close English translation is "worldview."

Western Buddhist Order. A highly successful European Buddhist missionary movement based in England.

Wicca. A vigorous *new religion that claims to practice *witchcraft. Members of Wicca say that traditional understandings of witchcraft as something that is evil are wrong and that they practice ancient healing arts and a pre-Christian religion. Wicca is a nature religion that involves *ritual practices built around the solar calendar and *polytheistic beliefs leading to the worship of various gods. Wiccans stress the healing nature of rituals and claim to seek the good of all. The best discussion of modern *neopaganism, including Wicca, is Ronald Hutton's *The Triumph of the Moon* (2000). Wiccans and other neopagans must not be confused with *Satanists, as often happens in pulp literature.

Wilber, Ken (1948-). Spiritual writer. Wilber is a self-taught college dropout who made it big as a spiritual writer and guru through books like *The Spectrum of Consciousness* (1977) and *Sex, Ecology, Spirituality* (1995). Clearly influenced by Frithjof *Schuon and other members of the *traditionalist school, his growing interest in politics reflects the classical fascist presentation of an alternative and more spiritual vision that lies between capitalism and communism. Whether Wilber is aware of his affinity to *fascism is unclear and even unlikely, although many aspects of his thought fit the *völkisch* mold.

witchcraft. A widespread system of beliefs and practices involving supernatural power and agencies thought to influence human affairs. Witchcraft is generally distinguished from *sorcery and takes many forms in different cultures. Sometimes the conscious action of individuals is involved; on other occasions witchcraft operates without conscious effort as a result of inherited powers or alien forces. Since the *Enlightenment, it has been usual to regard witchcraft as an irrational system of beliefs belonging to a primitive past. But anthropologists, beginning with Edward E. Evans-Pritchard (1902-1973), have shown that witchcraft involves a system of thought that, once accepted, follows a logical pattern. In the West popular belief in witchcraft died out during the seventeenth and eighteenth centuries, only to be revived in the late nineteenth century by Gerald *Gardner and other *occultists as a form of ritual *magic. It continues today with groups like *Wicca. In other parts of the world witchcraft has never died out, although its manifestation is very different due to the difference in social setting from modern witchcraft in the West.

Word of Wisdom. Dietary rules and advice for living proclaimed by Joseph *Smith and followed by *Mormons. It includes advice against drinking coffee, tea and alcoholic beverages.

worldview. *See* Weltanschauung.

Worldwide Church of God. A *new religious movement founded by
Herbert W. *Armstrong in 1933. Armstrong preached a form of *British Israelism supported by an *Arian Christology and denial of such
traditional Christian doctrines as the Trinity. The success of the movement began with Armstrong's innovative radio program, *The World
Tomorrow,* which was later adapted to television and was supported
by the free distribution of the magazine *The Plain Truth.* The church,
which experienced a major split in the 1970s, gradually moved toward
*orthodoxy following the death of its founder and finally accepted an
evangelical statement of faith in 1997.

Y

yin-yang. The Chinese philosophical theory that everything originates
from and depends on the interaction of two opposite and complemen-
tary principles that proceed from the great ultimate. Yin is earth—negative, passive, dark, female and destructive. Yang is heaven—light,
positive, male and constructive. Through the perpetual interplay of
yin and yang all things exist and are continually transformed.

yoga. A *Sanskrit term meaning "to yoke" that is used to describe a process of spiritual discipline or harnessing of physical and mental powers to attain self-control and ultimate *enlightenment. Generally *yoga*
means a system of *meditation that is essentially common to Buddhism, the Hindu tradition and *Jainism. It shares many associated assumptions, such as a view of *karma, *dharma and some notion of
*metempsychosis. The term also refers to one of the six schools of Hin-
du philosophy that teaches and utilizes the practice of yoga to attain
liberation, which is conceived of as a state of perfect isolation. *See also*
yogi; yogic religions.

Yogacaras. A school of Mahayana Buddhism. It subscribes to the idea
that consciousness alone is real, while objects of consciousness are not,
thus making *meditation rather than intellectual analysis the central
concern of the movement.

Yogananda, Paramahansa (1893-1952). Evangelist of the *Vedanta tradition. Yogananda adapted his teachings to a Western audience and settled in America. He drew extensively on the New Testament and
Bhagavad-Gita and wrote various books, including his *Autobiography
of a Yogi* (1946).

yogi. A practitioner of *yoga.

yogic religions. A term used to refer to those religious traditions where the practice of *yoga is the central experience and the doctrines associated with it, such as *karma, form the basis of belief. Yogic religions are the main rivals to *Abramic religions.

Yoshikazu, Okada (1901-1974). Also known as Okada Kotama, the founder of the Japanese new religion Sukyo Mahikari.

Young, Brigham (1801-1877). The St. Paul of Mormonism. Young assumed the leadership of those *Mormons who accepted polygamy after the death of Joseph *Smith. A brilliant leader, he created the Utah branch of the Church of Jesus Christ of Latter-day Saints. Despite his numerous gifts, he taught many strange doctrines now repudiated by his followers, including "blood atonement" and the "Adam-God" theory, which have proved troublesome for modern Mormon intellectuals.

Z

Zalman, Schneur, Rabbi of Liadi (1745-1812). Lithuanian Jewish leader and child prodigy who founded *Lubavitch Hasidism.

Zen Buddhism. A development of Japanese Buddhism that denies the reality of the external world and advocates mental and physical self-control as a path to *enlightenment. It is known for its use of the *koan and vivid stories about the sudden enlightenment of particularly holy men.

Zion Christian Church. African independent church. Commonly known as the ZCC, this *African independent church is the largest church in southern Africa with well over three million members, making it at least twice the size of any other church. It was founded in 1924 by Ignatius Lekganyane, who had been influenced by the work of John Alexander Dowie (1847-1907). Essentially *orthodox in theology, the church is charismatic with a strong emphasis on healing and *prophecy expressed in terms of traditional black cultural symbols. This enables it to act as an important modernizing force among upwardly mobile and recently urbanized people. Recently they have established branches in Europe and North America.